APPLIED RESEARCH DESIGN

APPLIED SOCIAL RESEARCH METHODS SERIES

Series Editors:
LEONARD BICKMAN, Peabody College, Vanderbilt University, Nashville
DEBRA J. ROG, Vanderbilt University, Washington, DC

APPLIED RESEARCH DESIGN

A Practical Guide

Terry E. Hedrick
Leonard Bickman
Debra J. Rog

SAGE Publications
International Educational and Professional Publisher
Thousand Oaks   London   New Delhi

For information address:

SAGE Publications, Inc.
2455 Teller Road
Newbury Park, California 91320

SAGE Publications Ltd.
6 Bonhill Street
London EC2A 4PU
United Kingdom

SAGE Publications India Pvt. Ltd.
M-32 Market
Greater Kailash I
New Delhi 110 048 India

Printed in the United States of America

Library of Congress Cataloging-in-Publication Data

Hedrick, Terry E. (Terry Elizabeth)
    Applied research design : a practical guide / Terry E. Hedrick,
Leonard Bickman, Debra J. Rog.
        p. cm. —(Applied social research methods series : 32)
    Includes bibliographical references and index.
    ISBN 0-8039-3233-2 (cl.)—ISBN 0-8039-3234-0 (pb)
    1. Social sciences—Research—Planning. 2. Social sciences—
Methodology. I. Bickman, Leonard, 1941- . II. Rog, Debra J.
III. Title. IV. Series: Applied social research methods series : v.
32.
H62.H3713 1993
300'.72—dc20   92-37330

93 94 95 96 10 9 8 7 6 5 4 3 2

Sage Production Editor: Tara S. Mead

Contents

Foreword

When my friends Terry Hedrick, Len Bickman, and Debra Rog asked me to write a foreword to their book, I was pleased but a little apprehensive. To my knowledge, there has never before been a book on *planning* applied research that is aimed at audiences who might never before have done such research. This means there is no easily available standard against which their work can be measured. But my own experience in planning and conducting applied research tells me that this book is absolutely first-rate, covering all the major points clearly and succinctly. It is also an important book. I am convinced that poorly planned applied research nearly always achieves poor results. It is true that one sometimes comes across poorly planned studies where the investigators were so creative they managed to make something out of nothing, often because of their willingness to reflect deeply on their own experiences "knee-deep in the muddy" and to write about them clearly. But these are exceptions. Most poorly planned research never gets completed, or once completed, it is consigned to a file drawer somewhere. Planning can help avoid these problems, even though it takes time and other resources to plan well.

The novelty of this book lies not only in bringing planning to the forefront of attention, but also in how planning is conceptualized. The book begins with the telling and relevant statement that "applied research planning is both a science and an art." It also reminds us on several occasions that planning is an iterative process and that replanning is sometimes called for as real-world events force deviations from the original plan. The authors particularly emphasize, however, that applied research planning is iterative in the more specific sense that the first draft of a question that has been generated after researchers have come to understand a general problem or issue still needs to be refined in the light of any feedback about the draft that interested parties to a policy or program might provide. Refining research questions over multiple occasions is crucial for enhancing their leverage whether the questions are descriptive, normative, correlative, or causal. Such planning will also help incorporate sponsors more deeply into the research and can increase the likelihood that the study results, once generated, will actually be used to change programs or policy.

Planning also has important technical aspects, and the authors rightly emphasize two of them. One is statistical power analysis. Again and again in the social sciences, we see studies being implemented that have no reasonable chance of detecting effects of the size expected given the sample sizes, variability in measures, and types of tests used. Indeed, meta-analysis would not have achieved its current high profile were it not for the omnipresence of statistically underpowered social research. The second technical issue the authors highlight concerns the study of program implementation, especially in those cases where causal questions of impact are paramount. The authors remind us how often programs are not implemented as they are supposed to be, and they remind us that this engenders the need to monitor implementation. Monitoring implementation in treatment groups needs little justification. But causal inferences are not about what goes on only in the intervention group. Rather, such inferences depend on the *contrast* between what was implemented in an intervention group compared to what was implemented in (usually) a control group. All too often, program evaluators have discovered that control group members undergo experiences that are more similar to the intervention experiences than had been planned, raising the need to monitor implementation among controls in exactly the same way as among experimentals. It is a strength of this book that it deals with planning to detect events for which one could not have planned.

The book also makes an eloquent case for studying resource issues during the planning stages of applied research. Under this heading the authors deal with issues of site selection, authorization, data collection, accessibility, and other sources of support, including human and financial support. There is a fine discussion of how to assess the human and material resources that will be needed at different times during the conduct of an applied research design so as to facilitate the management of data collection, analysis, and interpretation. Few basic researchers need to be as involved in such management issues, given how short-lived much of their research is and how few persons, institutions, and material resources are needed to pull off the work.

To judge from my own experience doing applied research, this is a fine book. It hits all the right nails squarely on the head and constructs a sturdy edifice upon which anybody could hope to erect his or her beginning career as an applied researcher.

—Thomas D. Cook
Northwestern University

Preface

Why this book—a text on planning and designing applied research? There are many textbooks available on research methods and statistics, and a significant body of program evaluation literature in both textbooks and journals. With all this material out there, it is only fair to ask, "Why another book?"

"To fill a gap about how really to conduct applied research" is the best answer we can offer. Every year during conferences or in other settings, we have spent time catching up with each other and discussing the "realities" of planning, designing, and implementing applied research projects. We have shared frustrations, ideas, and successes in ways that highlighted lessons learned, sometimes the hard way. We have found that we often use the content of these discussions later in teaching students and practitioners about how to conduct applied research in the complex and messy real world. Although we can find ample material to use in the classroom on design and methods, there appears to be a need for a text that can help the student make the transition from the classroom and laboratory to the rest of the world. This book, *Applied Research Design,* is intended to address this need at least partially.

Applied Research Design is written as an overview textbook for applied research classes and for practitioners. It assumes that students will have had previous exposure to the scientific method (i.e., the principles of basic research), but it recognizes that they may differ in their familiarity with quasi-experimental design, data collection methods, and statistics. The text is appropriate for individuals from backgrounds as diverse as business administration and psychology.

Much of the material deals with the processes of designing and planning research projects based on the more quantitative approaches. Reflecting the authors' backgrounds, there is a strong emphasis on program evaluation as examples of applied research. Though the text briefly reviews the technical aspects of designs and methods, it focuses on the practical considerations involved in developing research strategies that are high quality—in other words, credible, useful, and feasible. The presentation is purposefully brief, enabling instructors to supplement it with other texts as they deem appropriate. In particular, this book is intended to be the cornerstone of the Applied Social Research Methods Series. The book has been designed to complement the series texts dealing with research on special populations and settings and to dovetail with those providing much more detail on specific methods and measurement strategies. Therefore, where relevant, other volumes of the series are referenced.

We hope this book will provide students with an understanding of the need to be guided continually by the principles of research, rather than by prescribed designs and methods, as they endeavor to study problems and issues in dynamic environments. In addition, we hope this book will begin to fill the void for students and practitioners alike embarking on the field of applied social research.

Special thanks are in order to our reviewers, Mark W. Lipsey, Gary T. Henry, and Harry Havens; thanks also to Tom Cook, who both reviewed an earlier draft and graciously agreed to write the foreword.

1

The Nature of Applied Research

More and more frequently, public and private institutions are calling upon social scientists and other analysts to apply their research skills to assist in tackling real-world social problems. The requests are extremely varied. They include studying physicians' efforts to improve patients' compliance with medical regimens, determining whether drug use is decreasing at a local high school, providing up-to-date information on the operations of new educational programs or policies, evaluating the impact of environmental disasters, or even analyzing the likely effects of yet-to-be-tried programs to reduce teenage pregnancy. Researchers are asked to estimate the costs of everything from shopping center proposals to weapons systems, and to address the relative effectiveness of alternative programs and policies. Increasingly, applied researchers are asked to contribute to major public policy debates and decisions. These activities often challenge the skills researchers have learned in the classroom, because *the environment of applied research differs substantially from the environment of basic research.*

This text is designed to help the applied social research practitioner translate what he or she has learned in the classroom to the applied research environment. Applied research can encompass a wide range of approaches and contexts. As a result of the authors' collective backgrounds in social psychology, social experimentation, and program evaluation, the book clearly reflects these orientations, particularly in the examples used. Thus less attention is given to survey research, epidemiologic research, and research outside of human services. Yet we believe the basic framework of the book can be applied to a variety of applied research problems and situations.

In addition, many of the examples used are based on our work as *external* researchers and evaluators in a variety of contexts—university, state and federal government, and contract research firms. Again, we feel that much of the material in this volume is applicable to those who are in the role of internal evaluators; however, those readers interested in obtaining a greater understanding of the role of the internal evaluator are encouraged to review Love (1991).

We begin this first chapter by highlighting several of the differences between applied and basic research. We then stress a commonality: the need to engage in planning for research. Adequate planning is critical for conducting successful research, whether basic or applied. Planning to determine the focus of the research, planning to select the most appropriate design strategy, and planning to carry out the research are all stressed. At the end of this chapter, a research planning model is presented that will be used as the organizational framework throughout the text.

CONTRASTING BASIC AND APPLIED RESEARCH

Basic research is grounded firmly in the experimental method and has as its goal the creation of new knowledge about how fundamental processes work. In many ways, it is relatively protected research, allowed to build facts and theory incrementally in an environment generally of low stress and few outside influences or interruptions. Applied research also has its roots in the experimental method, but it uses scientific methodology to develop information aimed at clarifying or confronting an immediate societal problem. Its environment is often a messy one, with pressures for quick and conclusive answers, sometimes in very political contexts.

Outlining differences between basic and applied research is a risky undertaking. As quantitatively trained researchers, we are committed to the scientific method (i.e., designing rigorous research that aids in ruling out alternative explanations in drawing causal inferences), and we desire to carry out research that is technically sound. Highlighting differences between basic and applied research contexts can, at times, seem artificial to the reader or may create the impression that researchers in the applied community are "willing to settle" for something less than good science. This is not at all the case. Basic and applied research have many more commonalities than differences; however, their differences are critical for the applied researcher (and research consumer) to understand. A thorough understanding of the differences can help ensure that confusion and misunderstandings do not reign and that studies produce useful results as well as good science.

Basic and applied research differ in purposes, context, and methods. For ease of presentation we will discuss the differences as dichotomies; in reality, however, they fall on continua.

Differences in Purpose

One of the major differences between basic and applied research is the purpose, or the intentions, of the investigators or research sponsors (Nagi & Corwin, 1972). A summary of these differences is contained in Table 1.1 (adapted from Bickman, 1981).

The distinguishing feature of basic research is that it is intended to expand knowledge (i.e., to identify universal principles that contribute to our understanding of how the world operates). Thus it is knowledge, as an end in itself, that motivates basic research. Though it is often hoped that basic research findings will eventually be helpful in solving particular problems, such problem solving is not the immediate or driving goal of basic research. Applied research, in contrast, strives to improve our understanding of a specific problem, with the intent of contributing to the solution of that problem. Applied research also may result in new knowledge, but often on a more limited basis defined by the nature of an immediate problem.

Even though basic research is concerned much more with identifying universal principles, if one were to analyze the scope of basic and applied research studies, a much narrower scope would be found for most basic research investigations. Usually the basic researcher is investigating a very specific topic, and often this is a very tightly focused question. For example, what is the effect of white noise on the short-term recall of nonsense syllables? Or, what is the effect of cocaine use on fine motor coordination? The limited focus enables the researcher to concentrate on a single measurement task and to use rigorous design approaches that allow for maximum control of potentially confounding (disturbance) variables. In an experiment on the effects of white noise, the laboratory situation enables all other noise variables to be eliminated from the environment so that the focus can be exclusively on the effects of the variable of interest (i.e., the independent variable).

In contrast, the applied researcher often is faced with "fuzzy" issues underneath which lie multiple, often broad research questions, and he or she is asked to address them in a rather "messy" or uncontrolled environment. For example, what was the effect of the former First Lady Nancy Reagan's "Just Say No" drug abuse prevention program on high school students? Or, what are the causes of homelessness? In the first instance there are underlying questions of whether, and to what degree, the program was ever implemented. What was the program supposed to accomplish? What kinds of effects are relevant—knowledge of major drugs, use of drugs, attitudes toward drugs, and so forth?

Table 1.1

Comparison of the Purposes of Basic and Applied Research

Basic	Applied
Develop universal knowledge	Understand/address problems
Answer single questions	Answer multiple questions
Discover statistically significant relationships or effects	Discover practically significant relationships or effects

does difference make a difference?

Even when the questions are well-defined, the environment is a complex one, one that makes it difficult for the researcher to eliminate competing explanations (i.e., events other than the program could be likely causes for changes in attitudes or behavior). Obviously, there were many other drug-related initiatives under way at the same time as the "Just Say No" campaign. The number and complexity of measurement tasks and the complex real-world research settings pose major challenges for applied researchers. They also often necessitate making conscious choices (or trade-offs) concerning the relative importance of answering various questions and the degree of confidence necessary for each answer.

Finally, there are differences between the analytic goals of basic and applied research. Basic researchers generally are concerned most with determining *if an effect or causal relationship exists,* if it is in the direction predicted, and if it is statistically significant (e.g., if the differences observed in short-term recall in the presence and absence of white noise would not be expected by chance). Here the ultimate goal is to determine the existence or nonexistence of a universal principle (e.g., the interfering nature of noise distractions on short-term memory). In applied research, however, *both practical and statistical significance* criteria are important. Applied research also is concerned with determining if a causal relationship exists, but when studying causal relationships, applied researchers tend to study variables that they hope will produce societally significant results, effects that are of sufficient size to be meaningful. The focus of the research and the criteria for practical significance must be set in consultation with the stakeholders for the research—all parties with an investment in the research outcomes. From the research user's standpoint, discovering that a specific reading exercise is capable of increasing reading ability by only 5% may be very uninteresting and unhelpful. The user will be much more interested in determining whether students have acquired reading skills that are of practical significance and in whether the program appears to be replicable elsewhere.

These differences obviously have implications for research design planning, necessitating extensive work for the applied researcher in understanding the purpose of the endeavor and in focusing the study's research questions. It is critical, therefore, that the applied researcher understand the level of outcome that will be considered meaningful by key audiences and interest groups. For example, what level of reduced drug use is considered a practically significant outcome of the "Just Say No" drug program? As with basic research, it is equally important in applied research to establish causal connections between the intervention (independent variable) and the effects or outcomes that are statistically significant. Applied research has the added responsibility of determining if the level of outcome attained is important or trivial.

Differences in Context

It is in the research context that some of the biggest differences between basic research and applied research are found. A summary of these differences is presented in Table 1.2. The contrasts in Table 1.2 are oversimplified greatly; it is very easy to find exceptions to specific dimensions. The contrasts, however, highlight some of the most important differences that generally distinguish the two types of research.

Where the research occurs is itself a major factor in these differences. Basic research most typically is conducted in universities or similar academic environments, relatively isolated from the government or business worlds. Applied research also may be conducted in universities, but generally its contexts are more numerous and diverse. Applied research often is conducted in or focuses on federal and congressional agencies, state governments and legislatures, local governments, oversight agencies, professional or advocacy groups, private research institutions, foundations, business corporations and organizations, and service delivery agencies, among others. These settings, and their corresponding characteristics, can pose quite different demands on the applied researcher; these demands are discussed in Chapter 5.

University basic research usually is self-initiated. The idea for the study, the approach to executing it, and even the time line generally are determined by the researcher. This is the case even when funding is obtained from the government through the rather flexible mechanism of a federal grant. The researcher behaves fairly autonomously, setting the study scope and approach. If there is a research team, it generally

Table 1.2

Comparison of the Contexts of Basic and Applied Research

Basic	Applied
Academic settings	Government, foundation, business/ industrial settings
Self-initiated	Client initiated
Funded by grants	Funded by contracts
Solo researcher	Research team
Single discipline	Multidisciplinary
Lab or class	Field
Flexible	Inflexible
Lower cost sensitivity	Higher cost sensitivity
Less time pressure	More time pressure

will comprise persons the researcher chooses from the same or similar disciplines.

In contrast, the applied researcher often receives research questions from a client, and sometimes these questions are framed rather poorly and are not understood completely. The client is often in control, whether through a contractual relationship or by virtue of holding a higher position within the researcher's place of employment. The research most often is conducted by a research *team* rather than a solo researcher, and the teams are more likely to be multidisciplinary than in basic research, sometimes because of competitive positioning to win government research contracts or as a result of other disciplines already having established themselves as operators of programs or services. Moreover, the substance of applied research often necessitates a multidisciplinary team, particularly if there are multiple questions involving different areas of inquiry (economic, political, sociological, etc.). The team often must be composed of individuals who are familiar with the substantive issue (e.g., health care) as well as others who have expertise in specific methodological or statistical areas (e.g., economic forecasting).

Basic research is much more likely to be conducted within a controlled environment that is subject to close monitoring by the researcher, such as a university laboratory. The applied researcher usually cannot choose the environment for the research, for much of the data he or she needs will be found outside the laboratory. Lengthy negotiations are sometimes necessary even to obtain permission for access to the data. Maruyama and Deno (1992), for example, describe the negotiations that typically are necessary to gain access into schools to conduct research. Grady and Wallston (1988) describe similar issues in gaining and maintaining data access in health care settings, and such was also the case in the national evaluation of the Job Training Partnership Act (Doolittle & Traeger, 1990).

The reality is that the basic researcher operates in an environment with a great deal more flexibility, less need to let the research agenda be shaped by project costs, and less time pressure to deliver results by a specified deadline. Basic researchers sometimes even can undertake a multiyear incremental program of research that is intended to build theory in a systematic manner, often with supplemental funding and support from their universities. The applied researcher is much more limited in the actions that can be taken; must constantly be negotiating with the client in terms of project scope, cost, and deadlines; and may need to make conscious trade-offs in selecting a research approach that affects what questions will be addressed and how conclusively they will be addressed. Continuation funding is rare in applied research; if additional studies are desired, open competitive requests for proposals (RFPs) may be issued, and the researcher may compete along with other applicants again for funding. Even when the applied researcher manages to obtain support for a series of studies in the same general topic area, it often is not possible to continue further analyses of the data beyond those analyses directly supported by the contract. Furthermore, at times, issues of professional ethics may become relevant as researchers are faced with unreasonable demands for study conclusions, demands that cannot be met responsibly within the time frames or budgets set for individual projects.

More broadly speaking, research ethics are important in all types of research, basic or applied. When the research involves or affects human beings, the researcher must attend to a set of ethical and legal principles and requirements that can ensure that the research protects the interests of all those involved. Ethical issues arise in the selection and assignment of research participants to various experimental conditions or interventions; in the development of procedures for informed consent; in the development of strategies for protecting privacy, guaranteeing anonymity, and/or ensuring confidentiality; and in developing research procedures that are sensitive to and respectful of the specific needs of the population involved in the research. Ethical issues are most likely to arise when dealing with highly political and controversial social problems, in research that involves vulnerable populations (e.g., individuals with AIDS), and in situations where stakeholders have high stakes in the

outcomes of the research. When conducting federally sponsored research (usually under a contract, not a grant) that involves collecting
structured data from more than nine individuals or entities, the research
must be reviewed and cleared by the Office of Management and Budget
to ensure that the proposed data collection contains the requisite ethical
procedures and that it involves minimal risk and burden for the research
participants. Kimmel (1988) and Sieber (1992) review basic ethical
issues in social and behavioral research; Sieber also describes the role
of institutional review boards in assisting university-based researchers
in addressing these issues and in planning ethically responsive research.

The nature of the context in which applied researchers work highlights the need for both highly developed communication skills and
extensive expertise in research planning. Communication skills are
critical to working with clients and negotiating study objectives; sound
research planning skills also are essential. Applied researchers must
take deadlines as a given and then design research that can deliver
useful information within the constraints of budget, time, and staff
available. The key to quality work is to use the most rigorous methods
possible and to make intelligent and conscious trade-offs in scope and
conclusiveness. This does not mean that any information is better than
none, but that decisions about what information to pursue must be made
very deliberately, in conjunction with realistic assessments of the feasibility of executing the proposed research within the required time
frame. Chapter 5 describes the trade-offs that need to be considered in
making these decisions during the planning phases of research.

Differences in Methods

It should not be surprising that the previously described differences
in purpose and context result in differences in research approaches
(Table 1.3).

A key difference between basic and applied research is the relative
emphasis on internal and external validity. Whereas internal validity
(the extent to which a causal relationship can be established soundly)
is essential to both types of research, external validity (the extent to
which the study results are generalizable) is much more important to
applied research. Indeed, the likelihood that applied research findings
will be used is often a function of convincing policymakers that the
results are applicable to their particular setting or problem. For example, the results from a laboratory study of aggression using a bogus
shock generator and involving participants of different races are not

Table 1.3
Comparison of the Methods of Basic and Applied Research

Basic	Applied
Internal validity	External validity
Construct of cause	Construct of effect
Single level of analysis	Multiple levels of analysis
Single method	Multiple methods
Experimental designs	Quasi-experimental designs
Direct observations	Indirect observations

likely to be as convincing or as useful to policymakers who are confronting the problem of violent crime in the inner cities as the results from a well-designed survey describing the types and incidence of crime experienced by inner-city residents. Under many circumstances, it is thus appropriate to trade off internal validity (in this example even changing the study scope) in order to obtain greater external validity.

Second, basic research concentrates on the construct of cause. In laboratory studies the independent variable (cause) must be explicated clearly and not confounded with any other variables. If an investigator manipulates the perceived high or low credibility of a communicator, for example, in a study of attitude change, it is important that the manipulation clearly be one of credibility, and not be misinterpreted as being one of interpersonal attractiveness. On the other hand, it is rare in applied research settings that control over an independent variable is so clear-cut. For example, in program evaluations, the researcher typically cannot fully identify the specific aspects of a program that are responsible for an effect. This is attributable both to the complexity of many social programs and to the researcher's inability in most circumstances to manipulate different program features so as to discern differential effects. The applied researcher often must treat the program as a "black box," providing as much descriptive information as possible to enable others to replicate the entire program and its context at a later date. Methodological developments in implementation analysis (e.g., Brekke, 1987) promise to increase our ability to understand the "black box" and to measure the amount and nature of programmatic intervention received by each client (e.g., the "dose" of the program).

Applied research concentrates on the construct of effect. It is especially critical that the measures of effect be valid—in other words, that they accurately measure the constructs of interest. Often multiple measures are needed to assess the construct fully. Improvements in mental health, for example, may include measures of daily functioning, psychiatric status, and use of hospitalization. Moreover, measures of real-world outcomes are often mandatory; self-report and simple paper-and-pencil measures (e.g., self-report satisfaction with participation in a program) often are deemed to be inadequate for applied research. If attempts are being made to address a social problem, then real-world measures directly related to that problem are desirable. For example, it would not be advisable to conduct research on criminal justice programs designed to reduce criminal recidivism by just presenting descriptions of different intervention programs and asking individuals whether they thought these programs would work. More direct outcome measures, based on administrative records, would be required.

Third, there are differences in the levels of analysis performed in basic and applied research. Basic researchers often work at a single level of analysis, for example, measuring an individual's attitude or behavior. In contrast, the applied researcher usually needs to examine a specific problem at more than one level of analysis, studying not only the individual but often larger groups, such as organizations or even societies. For example, Fowler (1988), in an evaluation of a community crime-prevention project, not only examined individual attitudes and perspectives but also measured the reactions of groups of neighbors and entire neighborhoods to problems of crime. The added levels of analysis may require that the researcher be conversant with concepts found in a variety of disciplines (e.g., psychology, sociology, and political science) and to develop a multidisciplinary research team that can conduct this multilevel inquiry.

Research designs may differ as a function of both the context and the scope of the two types of studies. Because applied researchers often are given multiple questions to answer, because they must work in real-world settings, and because they often must have multiple measures of effects, they are more likely to use multiple research methods in a single study than are basic researchers. Although using multiple methods may be necessary to address multiple questions, it may also be a strategy used to approach a difficult problem from several directions, thus lending additional confidence to the study. Although it is desirable to use experimental designs whenever possible, and such has been done successfully, often the applied researcher is called in after a program or intervention is in place, which precludes the possibility of building random assignment into the allocation of program resources. Thus quasi-experimental studies often are used by applied researchers. The obverse, however, is rarer; quasi-experimental designs generally are not found in the studies published in basic research journals.

Finally, the types of data collected often differ in basic and applied settings. In the controlled environment of the laboratory, it is relatively easy to obtain and record observational data; however, in applied research in real-world settings, such direct observations often are not practical or economically feasible. Thus reliance frequently is placed on such other sources as self-reports of behavior, administrative records, and key informants, with efforts made to look for consistency or corroboration across measures.

In sum, the world of applied research often has more numerous and varied purposes, its context is less controllable, and its methods are more varied and more complex than research conducted in laboratory settings (Bickman & Henchy, 1971). These features make research planning activities especially critical. Although basic and applied research share a strong need for research planning, it easily can be argued that, given the greater complexity of the applied context, planning skills are even more important for applied researchers than for basic researchers.

A RESEARCH PLANNING MODEL

Applied research planning is both a science and an art. There are basic tenets to which one must adhere, there is a general order to the activities, and there are definite mistakes that can be made; however, good planning also involves creativity, flexibility, and responsiveness. Probably the most important concept for the new applied researcher to understand is that the process is an *iterative* one. The development of a research plan constantly is informed by new information that may result in changes to even the earliest working assumptions of the study—the specification of study questions.

The conduct of applied research can be viewed as consisting of two major phases: planning and execution (see Figure 1.1), encompassing four stages within those phases. In the planning phase, the researcher is concerned with defining the scope of the research (Stage I) and developing a research plan (Stage II). During execution, the research plan (design, data collection and analysis, and management procedures) is implemented fully and monitored (Stage III), followed by reporting and follow-up activities (Stage IV).

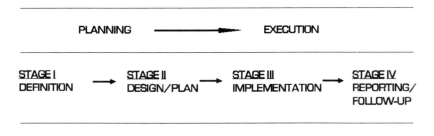

Figure 1.1. The Conduct of Applied Research

This book is focused on the first two stages of the research process. The organizing schema for the text generally follows the chronology of the design/planning process for applied research. We start with discussions of the need to define the research agenda and conclude at the point the student/practitioner is ready to begin full-scale implementation of the chosen strategy. Figure 1.2 summarizes the research planning approach advocated by this text, highlighting the iterative nature of the design process. Stage I of the research process begins by developing an understanding of the relevant problem/societal issue and involves working with research clients and other consumers to refine and revise study questions to make sure that they are both useful and researchable. This topic is covered in Chapter 2.

After developing potentially researchable questions, the investigator then moves to Stage II—development of a research design and plan. This stage involves multiple decisions and assessments: selecting the type of design (e.g., experimental vs. quasi-experimental; see Chapter 3) and the proposed data collection strategies (Chapter 4). Almost simultaneously with design and data collection decisions, the researcher must determine the resources necessary to conduct the study. This is the beginning of the operational planning for the research. It is also the area where social science academic education is most often deficient, and perhaps is one reason why academically oriented researchers may at times fail to deliver research on time. Chapter 5 summarizes the research planning process and provides several tools for breaking research execution into tasks and creating realistic time lines.

Before leaving Stage II, it is useful to assess the feasibility of carrying out the study design within the requisite time frame and available resources and to analyze the trade-offs of the design and other

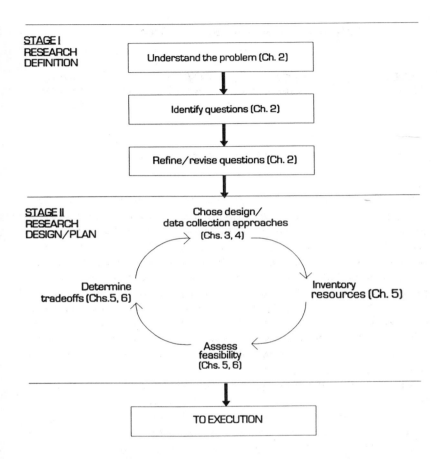

Figure 1.2. Applied Research Planning

planning decisions (Chapters 5 and 6). Feasibility testing may be as straightforward as pretesting a questionnaire or as complex as assessing the likelihood that local program officials will comply with study design requirements. In randomized designs, it may even be necessary to test local sites' ability to maintain the integrity of random assignment procedures (i.e., whether the clients or participants can be assigned randomly into treatment sites or no-treatment sites as originally proposed). Finally, as a last step, the researcher should outline the trade-offs (strengths and limitations) of the research plan, reaching a "go/no go" decision on its feasibility. The full plan, and analysis of any necessary trade-offs, should be discussed with the research consumer, and agreement should be reached on its appropriateness.

The planning activities in Stage II often will occur simultaneously. This is illustrated graphically in Figure 1.2 by showing these activities on a circular pathway that reverberates until a final research plan is developed. At any point in the Stage II process, the researcher may find it desirable to revisit and revise earlier decisions, perhaps even finding it necessary to return to Stage I and renegotiate the study questions or time line with the research client or funder. In fact, the researchers may find that the design that has been developed does not, or cannot, answer the original questions. Any such discrepancy needs to be reviewed and corrected together with the client before moving on to Stage III. The culmination of Stage II (also the culmination of this text) is a comprehensively planned applied research project, ready for full-scale implementation. With sufficient planning completed at this point, the odds of a successful study are improved significantly.

2

Defining the Focus of the Research

Both types of research, applied and basic, require significant time for conceptualization and planning activities. Unfortunately, applied researchers are much more likely than basic researchers to be pressured to produce research results quickly, and thus they may skimp on these activities. An inexperienced research sponsor or a novice researcher sometimes moves much too rapidly into data collection activities in order to meet deadlines for decision making. In many cases, abrupt start-ups prove foolhardy; good research typically requires substantial up-front work. Moving too quickly into the field makes it likely that the research will be unfocused and that, even if completed on time, it will yield irrelevant, poor, or even unusable data. In a few cases, scarce research resources may be consumed without the parties involved even having reached a consensus on the objectives of the research.

We believe that time devoted to study planning is justified by more definitive and useful results. Such efforts also often have a by-product of actually increasing the timeliness of results. Although time devoted to study planning activities may delay the start of data collection, once data collection begins it stands a better chance of proceeding smoothly. Moreover, time spent in developing a detailed research design, data collection, and analysis plan may improve the quality of the overall results. Rushed data collection efforts, on the other hand, may founder, forcing researchers back to the drawing board and thus costing more and consuming more calendar time.

In this chapter, we concentrate on the first stage of research planning: research definition. We advocate engaging in steps to clarify and refine the research scope prior to investing significant time and effort in design work. Among the steps involved in refining research are:

1. developing an understanding of the issue or problem underlying the research,
2. identifying the specific researchable questions, and
3. refining and revising the questions.

Time and effort devoted to these activities should increase the likelihood of successful execution of a research design and improve research utilization. Skimping on them can lead to serious problems (e.g., answering the wrong question, omitting key variables from the data collection plan, and missing the deadline for policy decisions). In concluding this chapter, we also discuss a key activity sometimes omitted from the applied research curriculum—the process of negotiating the scope of a project with research sponsors.

UNDERSTANDING THE PROBLEM/ISSUE

Although some applied researchers do not have a client to work with and thus have the luxury of setting their own research scope, many must struggle to decipher the "real" issues underlying their task. At times, the ambiguity may be unintended; even the primary research client may not have a clear understanding of the issue, only a feeling of discomfort that "something needs to be done" or investigated. At other times, the ambiguity may be a smoke screen. The research client may know the issue quite well but have a vested interest in (or already be convinced of) a particular outcome. For example, a CEO who has spent considerable resources on an employee training program clearly is invested in that program showing an increase in productivity. Thus the client may wish to persuade the researcher to "deliver" only positive information, not caring if the scope of the study is biased and the problem or issue remains incompletely studied.

To ensure that research is planned ethically and accurately, the researcher needs to educate himself or herself about the issue at hand. Strategies for gathering information include:

- holding discussions with the research clients or sponsors (agency, legislative member, foundation, business, organization, etc.) to obtain the clearest possible picture of their concerns;
- reviewing relevant literature (research reports, transcripts of legislative hearings, program descriptions, administrative reports, agency statistics, media articles, and policy/position papers by all major interested parties);
- gathering current information from experts on the issue (including all sides and perspectives) and major interested parties; and
- conducting information-gathering visits to sites of the program or problem to obtain a real-world sense of the context and to talk with persons actively involved in the issue.

These activities should enable the researcher to obtain a comprehensive and balanced view of the issue and to begin the process of defining the scope of the research. Obtaining clients' perspectives is essential, especially understanding any ideas they may have for developing action-oriented recommendations (see Majchrzak, 1984), because the research may need to be developed to inform these kinds of choices. Understanding the client's perspective also is useful for understanding the political playing field and thus avoiding becoming an advocate for either side before the data are analyzed.

Literature reviews can provide an historical context for the issue. Many social policy issues are cyclical; remedial approaches may have been tried before and evaluated. A literature review can both inform the researcher as to where others have been with this problem and help him or her avoid conceptual or methodological mistakes of the past. Reviews can include annual program or agency reports, grant applications, and any special reports, as well as more traditional academic literature. The review also may provide guidance on the state-of-the-art procedures and methods that have been used in the area, not to mention some insights into the resources that may be needed to conduct the study. In other areas, particularly where a number of studies have been conducted, it may be desirable to include the development of an integrated literature review (see Cooper, 1989) or a meta-analysis (Rosenthal, 1991) as a separate research product. Meta-analysis is a tool to cumulate evidence quantitatively regarding the importance of the effects of any independent variable. It often is conducted as a study in its own right, although it can be a preliminary study.

In some cases, the literature review may be the first clue that a secondary data set may exist that can be used to perform the study, rather than starting from scratch with new data collection. Stewart and Kamins (in press) provide a review of some major sources of secondary data (e.g., census data) that can be used in a variety of investigations.

Despite the need for gathering information on the historical context, a literature review is no substitute for discussions with current experts on the issue. The terms of debate in a field change, new information emerges that has not yet been published, and other information sometimes is obtained from these discussions that is enlightening about the "reality" of the problem. These discussions may also be preliminary steps to forming a research advisory group representative of the full range of views on the issue.

Finally, preliminary site visits, whether to housing projects or stock exchanges, are well worth the effort. These information-gathering visits give a rich picture of the issues and sometimes change the researcher's overall understanding of the problem, potentially affecting not only the selection of research questions but also measurement, design, data collection, and analysis choices. Timely interviews with experts and site visits also can help to identify specific sensitivities of the study—the need to involve affected community groups (e.g., neighborhood commissions), the need to begin thinking about procedures that may be necessary to preserve confidentiality of respondents, or the need to obtain continuing advice on how to do research with certain populations or in certain settings, such as among Hispanic populations (Marin & Marin, 1991) or persons with mental illness (Dworkin, 1992), or in educational (Maruyama & Deno, 1992) and health care settings (Grady & Wallston, 1988).

When issues are especially difficult to clarify, several additional tools are available to the applied researcher to generate new information and/or achieve group consensus on a study scope. These can include such qualitative techniques as participant observation (Jorgensen, 1989), ethnographic methods (Fetterman, 1989), and other observational research tools. Small-group techniques such as nominal group technique and the Delphi technique may be used with issue experts to obtain their help in developing a meaningful agenda for the research (see Moore, 1987). Focus groups, a technique originally used in market research for obtaining consumer reactions to new products, also can be very useful, particularly when making site visits (see Stewart & Shamdasani, 1990) to understand how a program operates and what participants view as the real issues. An added benefit from these discussions is the utility of the information they may provide for later design of data collection instruments. Because focus group discussions typically are recorded, the researcher can use the data to help design survey or interview instruments that are phrased in the participants' own vocabulary.

Through these "scoping activities," the researcher should have a thorough grounding in the problem, the specific interests of the research sponsors, and some notion of the particular constraints or boundaries that will affect the research (time deadlines, resources available, skill required for specific research duties, etc.). After obtaining this thorough grounding, the researcher is ready to work with the client in both fleshing out a conceptual framework of the key problem and the study approach and developing the specific research questions.

DEVELOPING A CONCEPTUAL FRAMEWORK

All studies, whether it is acknowledged or not, are based on a conceptual framework that specifies the variables of interest and the expected relationships among them. The framework may be relatively straightforward or complex, as in the case of impact studies positing several kinds of effects. Social science theory may serve as the basis for the conceptual framework in some studies. For example, theories of cognitive development may drive investigations of children's learning abilities. Other studies may be based not on formal academic theory but on statements of expectations of how policies or programs are purported to work. Bickman (1987, 1990) and others (e.g., Chen & Rossi, 1992) have written extensively about the need for and usefulness of program theory to guide evaluations.

Much of the information obtained from reviewing the literature and from talking with experts during the problem identification task is relevant here. These kinds of activities enable the researcher to identify the important variables and to determine the expected causal relationships. The researcher should not be surprised if the various information sources do not always agree. If a general consensus is not evident, it is important at this stage to retain information on all parties' views. Again, this is especially necessary when the topic under study is highly controversial and when clients have a vested interest in the research results supporting their views. A key aspect of applied research is its neutrality. Neutrality is derived from a balanced research agenda, and this research agenda is based on the completeness of the conceptual framework underlying the study.

One mechanism for refining the focus, particularly in program or policy evaluations, is the development of a logic model to display the logic of the program—that is, how the program goals, resources, activities, and outcomes link together (Rog, in press; Rog & Huebner, 1992). The model can be used as a vehicle for the researcher to communicate his or her understanding of the program and to determine how the evaluation should be focused. The use of the logic model in program research is based on the work of Wholey and others (e.g., Wholey, 1987) in describing and displaying the underlying theory of a program. Rog and Huebner (1992) further discuss how existing formal theory can be used to structure the development of an intervention and the subsequent evaluation of the intervention's effectiveness.

For descriptive and correlational studies, the conceptual framework is likely to be fairly simple. The key for these types of studies is to identify all variables necessary to describe "what is" adequately or to determine whether certain factors covary. Table 2.1 lists examples of variables that might be useful for studying vocational computer training. These variables refer to the training organization, the nature of the training, the training methods, and the environmental context.

Consultation with area experts, visits to selected programs, and review of training plans can be used to make sure that all important variables are included. It is desirable to conduct meetings with research clients during the process of developing the conceptual framework to check that the research will collect information on all areas they deem critical. Also, for correlational studies a further step is required. Here the researcher must specify whether the expected correlation is positive (e.g., whether the cost of the program is expected to increase with increases in the duration of the training, and vice versa), or negative (e.g., the cost of the program is expected to decrease with increases in the duration of the training, and vice versa). If the expectation is that method of instruction is correlated with the unemployment rate, the conceptual framework should include a statement such as the following:

Computer literacy students in high-unemployment areas will be more likely to receive classroom training and less likely to receive on-the-job training than students in low-unemployment areas.

In other words, the researcher hypothesizes that the proportion of students spending time in the classroom is correlated positively with the unemployment rate.

For impact studies, the conceptual framework is more complex. In addition to specifying the key variables, it is necessary to specify the hypothesized direction of causal relationships. Example 1 of Figure 2.1 displays a simple conceptual framework for a study of the effects of computer training programs, considering all types of training as one treatment or intervention.

The framework can take many forms, depending on its complexity and on the nature of the audience. Example 2 of Figure 2.1 displays a framework for a relative effectiveness evaluation comparing the effects of classroom versus on-the-job training. In both examples, the program appears on the left side of the diagram, with anticipated effects on the right side. The horizontal arrows refer to the direction of *causation* (i.e., what causes what) and the plus and minus signs refer to the direction

Table 2.1

Conceptual Framework for Descriptive/Normative/Correlational
Studies (examples of variables for vocational computer training)

Training Organization	Nature of Training	Training Methods	Environmental Context
Time in Operation (months):	Content:	Mode:	County Size:
	Hardware	Classroom	< 20,000
< 6	DOS	On-the-job	20,001-50,000
6-12	Word processing	Self-paced	50,001-100,000
13-24	(beginning/	Mixed	100,001-300,000
25-60	advanced)		300,001-600,000
> 60	Spreadsheets		> 600,000
	Graphics		
	Desktop publishing		
Service Deliverer:	Intensity (hours/week):	Class Size:	Employment Rate:
CBO	< 5	Individual	< 3%
Community college	5-16	2-6	3.1%-4%
For-profit firm	17-32	7-20	4.1%-5%
Nonprofit firm	33-39	> 20	5.1%-6%
	> 39		> 6%
	Duration (months):		Eligible Population:
	< 2		% female
	2-6		% minority
	7-12		% H.S.
	> 12		graduate
			Age
	Cost:		
	< $100/person		
	$101-$200		
	$201-$500		
	$501-$700		
	$701-$900		
	> $900		

of the expected *effect* (i.e., whether training is expected to increase or decrease subsequent earnings). The ordering of variables refers to the expected sequencing of effects. For example, training is expected to

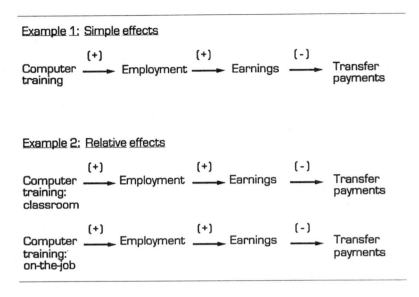

Figure 2.1. Sample Conceptual Framework for Impact Study

increase the probability of subsequent employment, and the increased employment then is expected to increase students' earnings. Increased earnings should then decrease receipt of government transfer payments such as unemployment insurance, Aid to Families with Dependent Children (AFDC), or food stamps.

Whenever possible, it is desirable to collect data that address the complete conceptual framework; however, resources will not always be available to do so. In this case, it is important that the decisions on what data to omit are made consciously and in conjunction with the client. Because omitting part of the framework also has the potential to bias the study's scope, it is also important to review these decisions carefully. For example, parties interested primarily in the quality of life for the students in the training program might argue that even if earnings increase, the decrease in transfer payments (AFDC, food stamps, and unemployment insurance) and additional work expenses incurred ultimately will result in the students' families having less disposable income. None of the frameworks in Figure 2.1 include the variable of disposable income. Figure 2.2 shows a more complete framework incorporating this additional variable.

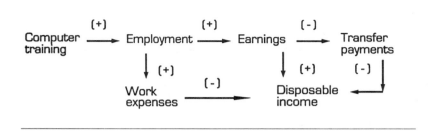

Figure 2.2. Revised Conceptual Framework for Impact Study

Reports should present the complete conceptual framework and then specify what part of it is addressed by the study and what part is not. This ensures that the credibility of the study is maintained, and that the consumer of the research clearly understands any limitations of the study scope.

IDENTIFYING THE RESEARCH QUESTIONS

As was noted in Chapter 1, one of the major differences between basic and applied research is that the basic researcher is often more autonomous than the applied researcher. Basic research, when externally funded, typically is conducted through the relatively unrestrictive grant mechanism; applied research more frequently is funded through contracts that have specified deadlines and products—specified "deliverables" such as design papers, data collection instruments, Office of Management and Budget (OMB) clearance packages (i.e., clearance to review the burden of the research on participants and the suitability of the research to federal priorities), analysis plans, and reports. There is usually a "client" or sponsor who specified (or at least guided) the research agenda and requested the research results. The identity of the real client may not be obvious; it may not be the funding agency but a congressional committee that is interested in the study. Often there are multiple stakeholders to a study (Bickman & Rog, 1986).

Usually both the client and the researcher have a base of expertise relevant to the project. The client (e.g., a government agency, legislative body, nonprofit agency, or private business) initially may have greater substantive or programmatic expertise about the issue or program under study; the researcher brings technical expertise and conceptual or theoretical skills to the project. This means that the questions to be addressed by an applied study tend to be posed by someone other than the primary researcher, often by nontechnical persons in nontechnical language. Differences in knowledge bases and vocabularies naturally create opportunities for confusion. The usual problems that occur when people try to discuss complex issues are compounded by differences in how clients and researchers define terms. One of the first activities of applied researchers and clients should be to develop a common understanding of the research agenda—the research questions. Phrasing study objectives as questions is desirable in that it leads to more focused discussion of the type of information that is needed. It also makes it more likely that key terms (e.g., welfare dependency, drug use) will be operationalized and defined clearly. Later, after additional information has been gathered and reviewed, the parties will need to reconsider whether these questions are the right questions or whether it is possible, with a reasonable degree of confidence, to obtain answers for these questions within the available resource and time constraints.

Table 2.2 provides a useful taxonomy for categorizing research questions (adapted from U. S. General Accounting Office, 1984a). The four major categories—descriptive, normative, correlative, and impact (causal)—can help refine the research agenda of almost any study.

Descriptive Questions

Descriptive questions are "what is" and "what was" inquiries. Purely descriptive questions are the most straightforward questions. They generally require information on the characteristics of some entity (e.g., the nature of a problem, the objectives of a program, the needs of a population). The data to be gathered are descriptive in nature, designed to present a picture of what exists or what is happening. An example of a simple descriptive research question is, "What training methods are being used in computer literacy programs?" An example of a simple descriptive research result is, "Nationally, one third of the vocational education students in computer literacy programs received classroom training on stand-alone personal computers; one third received training

Table 2.2
Types of Applied Research Questions (with examples)

Descriptive
- What training methods are being used in computer literacy education?
- How prevalent is drug use among high school students?
- What is the average percentage tip given in restaurants, overall and for dining parties of 2, 4, and 8 persons?

Normative
- Are the methods being used in computer literacy education in conformance with state vocational education standards?
- How well run is the education program?
- How serious is the drug abuse problem in local high schools?
- Does the average tip in restaurants equal the 15% of check recommended by the National Restaurant Association?

Correlative
- Is there any relationship between local economic conditions and the types of training services offered by vocational education agencies?
- What is the relationship between gender, age, academic performance, and high school drug use?
- Is there an association between size of dining party and percentage tip given in a restaurant?

Impact
Simple effects
- Does participation in computer literacy programs increase the probability of subsequent employment?
- Do lack of knowledge about drugs and easy access to drugs increase teenagers' likelihood of abusing drugs?
- Does size of dining party affect tipping generosity in restaurants?

Relative effects
- Which type of training, classroom or on-the-job, is most effective in increasing the probability of employment?
- What are the relative contributions of two factors, lack of knowledge about drugs and easy access to drugs, in leading teenagers to abuse drugs?
- Which factor, size of dining party or amount of alcohol consumed, is more influential on tipping generosity in restaurants?

SOURCE: The taxonomy of types of questions is adapted from terminology used in U. S. General Accounting Office, *Designing Evaluations: Methodology Transfer Paper 4*, Program Evaluation and Methodology Division, July 1984.

on-the-job from private firms; and one third obtained their training from self-paced computer-based courseware." Not all descriptive questions, however, are easy to address. Consider the question, "How many homeless children are there in the United States?" The question is purely descriptive, but the execution of such a research study would be extremely difficult, involving a sound understanding of the problem and context to enable the development of appropriate data collection methods and procedures, such as client tracking procedures, counting procedures, and so forth.

Normative Questions

Normative questions pose an additional information requirement. Besides requiring descriptive information on the characteristics of an entity, they require comparing those characteristics to a standard. They ask, "What is the difference between what is (or what was) and what should have been?" The standard may be based on any one of a number of sources—legislative objectives, professional standards, program goals, or any other set of a priori criteria. An example of how pure descriptive objectives can be expanded to normative questions is as follows: "Are the methods being used in computer education programs in conformance with state vocational education standards?" An example of a descriptive-normative research result is,

> Across the state, one third of the vocational education students in computer training received classroom training on office machinery; one third received training on-the-job from private firms; and one third received self-paced computer-based training through courseware. Thus vocational education computer training programs fell substantially below the state standards requiring at least half of the students to obtain their training in the workplace.

As can be seen from this example and the Table 2.2 illustrations, normative questions often are used for the monitoring of a program or studying policy implementation.

In the preceding example, the choice of the standard for evaluating implementation was easy. State standards for vocational education existed in writing, and data on actual training operations could be compared to the standards to identify any discrepancies. In other cases, the researcher may have to struggle to develop a standard. Ideally, the activity takes place during the initial scoping phase of the research.

Questions such as "How *serious* is the drug abuse problem in local high schools?" or "How *well* are community development block grants operating in the state of Ohio?" require researchers to develop criteria for a "serious" problem or "well"-operating grant programs. Methods of developing standards include reviewing prior research, reviewing statements of legislative intent, and discussions with recognized experts. Development of the standards may even become an activity of the research itself, involving data gathering to determine the incidence of various events in similar geographic areas or circumstances.

The most difficult situation arises when there is disagreement as to standards. For example, many parties may disagree as to what defines *serious* drug abuse—is it defined best as 15% or more of students using drugs weekly, 5% or more using hard drugs such as cocaine or PCP monthly, students beginning to use drugs as young as seventh grade, or some combination of the dimensions of rate of use, nature of use, and age of user? Likewise, parties interested in community development block grants may disagree as to the optimum use of such grants. In such cases, standards may be both multidimensional and controversial. Applied researchers should, to the degree possible, attempt to achieve consensus from research consumers in advance of the study (e.g., through advisory groups) or at least ensure that their studies are able to produce data relevant to the standards posited by all potentially interested parties. This is particularly important in areas in which small differences in results are important and the need for a high level of study precision is required. The issue of research precision and statistical power is discussed in Chapter 4.

Correlative Questions

Correlative questions ask whether certain entities are related, that is, to what degree do they covary either positively (as X increases, so does Y) or negatively (as X increases, Y decreases)? Correlational data only indicate whether there is a relationship between two or more variables, and the strength and direction of that relationship. An example of a correlational question is "Is there any relationship between local economic conditions and the kinds of training programs offered by vocational education agencies?" An example of a correlational result is "The higher the local unemployment rate, the more likely it is that vocational education programs use classroom-based training rather than on-the-job experience with local employers."

When one of the variables (e.g., X) is a manipulable variable, determining the existence of a correlation is the *first* step in establishing a cause-and-effect relationship (whether X causes Y). Unfortunately, correlational results sometimes are interpreted erroneously as *establishing* cause. In the preceding example, research consumers might mistakenly leap to the conclusion that high unemployment rates lead local service agencies to offer classroom training rather than on-the-job training. Several alternative explanations, however, are possible. For example, local agencies in high-unemployment areas may prefer to offer on-the-job training opportunities but may find it difficult to develop agreements with local businesses in hard economic times. Thus the configuration of services may not be the result of a choice by the agency but instead be imposed externally. A third factor also may be operating; further investigation might indicate that areas with high unemployment are generally urban areas and are historically more likely than other areas to contract out training to nonprofit community-based organizations. These nonprofit organizations historically may have operated extensive classroom training programs. In this case, historical organizational ties help explain the selection of training methods, and high unemployment rates are irrelevant or spurious as a cause.

Researchers asked to address correlational questions should engage in clarifying discussions with clients to determine if their research objectives are truly correlational, or if they actually wish to make causal inferences. There are indeed instances when the questions may be entirely correlative without any causal implications. For example, one may want to know the correlation between age and unemployment to know how best to target job training programs.

Confusion between correlational and causal research objectives is one of the most frequent sources of misunderstandings between applied researchers and research clients. If the client is, in fact, interested in understanding the causal relationship between two or more variables, then the applied researcher needs to work with him or her in developing researchable impact questions.

Impact Questions

Impact questions ask what causes (or caused) what. They ask not only whether two or more entities covary, but whether a change in one is found to cause a change in the other (i.e., whether causal attribution is possible). Examples of impact questions are "Does participation in computer literacy training increase the probability of subsequent employment?" or "Which type of training—classroom, self-paced computer-based, or on-the-job—is more effective in increasing the probability of subsequent employment?" The first question is an _absolute_ effectiveness question. The second question is a _relative_ effectiveness question; it compares the strength of three alternatives (in this case, three types of training approaches) in achieving the same effect. An example of an impact research result is: "Classroom and self-paced computer-based modes of computer training increased the probability of subsequent employment by 10%, whereas on-the-job training increased the probability of subsequent employment by 22%."

Answering impact questions requires the development of a comparison base, that is, an estimate or measurement of what would have been the case if the causal entity had not been present. In the education example, it is necessary to estimate or measure the rate at which persons similar to those participating in the computer literacy training obtained employment. A comparison of their employment experiences with those of persons receiving training services is the basis for estimating program effectiveness.

To answer the relative effectiveness question, it is essential that the students receiving the various modes of training (classroom, self-paced computer-based, and on-the-job training) be comparable. Otherwise, any differences between them, such as prior education or experience, could influence the probability of employment and thus distort the estimate of effectiveness. In addition, it is also necessary to establish a comparison base of what would have happened to similar students if they had not participated in any of the training activities. Otherwise, it is not possible to determine whether the employment outcomes of any of the modes of training were better than would have been obtained without services. As will be discussed in Chapter 3, the best method for establishing comparison bases and estimating the relative effectiveness of different conditions (e.g., training methods) is random assignment to these conditions; however, it is sometimes possible to produce credible estimates of effects through nonexperimental or statistical approaches.

Sometimes impact research questions will require comparison to a standard, much like normative descriptive questions. For example, authorizing legislation may specify criteria for a program's success. State standards for vocational education programs could specify that computer training services will be judged to be successful only if they achieve an increase in subsequent employment of at least 20%. By this criterion, classroom training's observed effect of a 10% increase in employment in the above example would be judged as a failure, as would that of self-paced computer-based training. On-the-job training, found to result in a 22% increase in employment, would be judged as a success. Even when such standards are not specified, it is advisable to discuss with clients their expectations for the size of effects and what they would consider to be "practically significant" prior to designing the research. This creates a common understanding of how the research will be interpreted and is essential to the design of studies. The size of effect a researcher or client wishes to detect will be a major factor in determining the size of required samples (e.g., number of students surveyed). It is also important to ascertain the duration of the expected effect (i.e., whether it is an immediate effect of short life or a more gradual effect that is expected to persist). The classic mistake is one of estimating a short-term cost savings from a new program or policy only to miss the fact that the eventual longer-term cost becomes overwhelming.

The practical size of change can be difficult to establish. Various substantive areas currently are struggling with this issue. For example, there is heated discussion concerning the clinical significance of changes occurring in psychopathology (Jacobson & Truax, 1991). Such discussions across a range of areas could help clarify how we approach designing studies.

Other Types of Questions

Although the taxonomy of questions described previously constitutes the core of applied research, it by no means encompasses all applied research. For example, at this point, we have used this taxonomy solely to address current or past conditions, such as the current severity of the national youth drug abuse problem or the past effectiveness of a computer literacy education program. Yet applied researchers are sometimes asked to project results (e.g., to forecast the severity of youth drug abuse in the 1990s, or to estimate the feasibility of implementation and effectiveness of a proposed program). These latter questions are *prospective* questions; they demand that the researcher use whatever systematic information he or she can array to predict future states. Although it is possible to categorize these prospective questions within the taxonomy as descriptive, correlative, and impact questions, they can require quite different design and analytic approaches. Because of space limitations, we have chosen not to include prospective questions within the scope of this text. Interested readers are referred to recent texts on policy analysis and forecasting (Nagel & Neef, 1979; Weimer & Vining, 1992).

Another variation on the taxonomy involves *cost questions* such as those related to simple cost, cost-benefit analysis, or cost-effectiveness. These questions require translating research results into dollars. Simple cost questions can be descriptive; for example, how much does it cost to provide a specific service? Or, in a more complicated vein, a researcher may be asked to describe the severity of the youth drug abuse problem in terms of dollar costs to society (e.g., medical costs, education costs, lost productivity). This appears, at first glance, to be a straightforward cost question, but it is very difficult to study.

Cost-benefit approaches usually are used by economists. Using this approach involves translating both the benefits and costs of a program or policy into dollars and then calculating a ratio. In general, this approach is used to answer questions about whether the dollar benefits of a program justify its costs. For example, using our vocational education program example, one might ask whether the government's cost of operating computer training programs is repaid within 2 years by decreases in transfer payments and increases in income taxes paid after participants obtained employment. Cost-benefit questions often are posed from multiple perspectives—those of society, the government (federal, state and/or local), and program participants—in order to ensure that all parties' circumstances are considered.

The last type of cost question concerns cost-effectiveness. The literature has provided widely different definitions of this type of question in the last few years (Levin, 1983; Thompson, 1980). The most straightforward way to define a cost-effectiveness approach, however, is to present it as translating program costs into dollars but leaving program results in the form of the original measures. For example, again using the vocational education program, one might ask how much it costs the government to increase the net employment rate of training participants by 15%. Or, what is the additional government cost per additional training participant employed full-time 1 year later? Here employment rates and persons employed remain in their original metric and are juxtaposed against program costs.

Cost questions and approaches for answering them are far from simple, and they frequently require making fairly wide-ranging assumptions, using both optimistic and pessimistic economic assumptions and providing a range of results. A controversy of many years duration has raged over the degree of utility and conclusiveness of these approaches. At the very least, however, it does appear that descriptive cost analysis and financial information are important aspects of many applied research studies. Interested readers are referred to the more specialized literature for additional information about the controversy and specific cost analysis methods (Thompson, 1980).

Clarifying the Study Questions

Several examples of descriptive, normative, correlative, and impact questions are provided in Table 2.3. In discussing the research agenda with clients, multiple types of questions may be identified. Especially in a nonacademic environment, researchers frequently will be asked to produce comprehensive information both on the implementation (what is, and the difference between what is and what should be) and the effects (what caused what) of a specific policy or program. These broad research agendas pose significant challenges for study planning in terms of allocating data collection resources among the various study objectives.

In clarifying and setting the research agenda, researchers should guard against biasing the scope of the research. The questions left unaddressed by a study can be as important or more important than the questions answered. If the research addresses only questions likely to support the position of one political entity in a controversy and fails to develop information relevant to the concerns voiced by other interested parties, the research will be seen as biased even if the results produced are judged to be sound and conclusive. Thus to the degree possible, the research agenda should be as comprehensive as is necessary to address the concerns of all parties. If resource constraints limit what questions may be addressed, at minimum the researcher should state explicitly what would be necessary for a comprehensive study and how the research meets or does not meet those requirements.

A study performed by the U.S. General Accounting Office (GAO; 1984b, 1985) for the House Committee on Ways and Means illustrates the value of maintaining balance in the research agenda (Hedrick & Shipman, 1988). The committee asked the GAO to review the effects of changes made in 1981 to the Aid to Families with Dependent Children (AFDC) program. These changes tightened financial eligibility and benefit rules for working welfare parents and resulted in the disqualification of many AFDC families from benefits. Advocates of the changes argued that the previous AFDC rules had deterred families from achieving welfare independence and had paid out benefits to families that already had sufficient financial resources. Tightening the rules was also judged desirable in terms of reducing program costs in a time of fiscal constraints. Opponents argued that the changes would discourage these

Table 2.3
Examples of Primary and Subordinate Questions

Primary:	How prevalent is drug use among high school students?
Subordinate:	What percentage use cocaine at least weekly?
	What percentage use marijuana daily?
	What percentage sell drugs to other students?
Primary:	How many homeless children are there in the United States?
Subordinate:	How many are below age 12?
	What percentage are black, white, Hispanic, and Asian?
	What percentage are living in urban areas?
Primary:	Is NASA making optimum use of its computer facilities?
Subordinate:	What percentage of time are the facilities idle?
	How much time is consumed by maintenance and administrative tasks?
	Are rates charged outside parties competitive?
Primary:	Did the computer training literacy program increase employment for high school youth?
Subordinate:	Were there different effects for male and female students?
	What kinds of jobs or subsequent education opportunities did they obtain?
	What was the cost per student?

families from working; that many of these families would cease to work in the future and become increasingly dependent on welfare (thus increasing program costs); and that even if families continued to work, their quality of life would be reduced greatly. Designing a study to address changes in "quality of life" for AFDC families losing benefits necessitated adding major survey resources to the GAO study; however, answering only the questions concerning effects on work effort and program costs could have been seen as biased. The concerns of major opponents to the legislative changes would have not been addressed. Thus the GAO adopted a comprehensive research agenda encompassing all major areas of concern.

Ideally, the development of the conceptual framework should occur simultaneously with the identification of the research question. Once the conceptual framework has been agreed upon, the researchers can refine the study questions further—grouping questions and identifying which are primary and subordinate questions (see Table 2.3). Areas to clarify include on what time frame the data should be based (e.g., program enrollees in fiscal years 1991 and 1992; high school seniors in the fall of 1992), how far the client wants to generalize (e.g., to program enrollees nationally; to high school seniors in Chicago, New York, and Philadelphia), and what subgroups the client wants to know about (e.g., male and female program enrollees; Hispanic, white, black, and Asian high school seniors). The level of specificity should be very high at this point, enabling a clear agreement on what information items will be produced. These discussions with research clients many times take on the flavor of a negotiation: a negotiation of research scope.

NEGOTIATION OF STUDY SCOPE

Communication with the research client (the sponsor and all interested parties) is stressed throughout this text. To ensure maximum utilization of results—and accurate utilization—the authors urge continuous interaction with research clients, from the initial discussions of the problem to recommendations and follow-up. The following communication strategies are advocated with respect to the planning activities:

- An initial meeting should be held with the client to develop a common understanding of the research questions, the client's time frame for study results, and anticipated uses for the information. This meeting also can be used to discuss preliminary ideas regarding a conceptual framework for the study. It is the opportunity to explore whether the client expects only to be provided information on study results or whether the client anticipates that the researcher will offer recommendations for action. It also is the opportunity to determine whether interim findings will be provided to the client as the study progresses.
- For externally funded research, it is also important to reach a tentative agreement on the amount of funds or resources that will be available to support the research. Chapter 5 describes how to compute a budget, but it is necessary to know what the client thinks about the size of the project. Cost considerations will determine the scope of the project, and they need to be considered even while identifying and reviewing the research questions. It is critical that ballpark figures be agreed to early in the negotiation process. In federal studies, however, it is likely that the cost of the study has been determined through the competitive RFP process prior to any direct personal contact with the research client. The client will no doubt have had a role in this process, but it is likely to have been filtered through the formal negotiation process required in federal contract procedures.

- Following the researcher's review of literature relevant to the proposed study and an initial assessment of resources, a second meeting should be held to refine the research questions and to discuss potential research approaches under consideration to answer these questions, as well as study limitations. This is the opportunity to introduce constraints into the discussion regarding available resources, time frames, and any trade-offs contemplated regarding the likely conclusiveness of answers to the questions.
- A third meeting should be held to reach agreement on the proposed study approach. If some uncertainty remains, the researcher may find it useful to offer alternative approaches, specifying for the client what will be obtained from each approach and the level of effort and time required. The goal of this meeting should be for the client and the researcher to reach agreement on a proposed approach. It should be stressed that it will be necessary for the researcher to investigate further the feasibility of the chosen approach (see Chapter 4) in the field, and that if changes are necessary further meetings will be held to discuss the implications of these changes.

Most research clients want to support sound, well-executed research and are sympathetic to researchers' needs to preserve the integrity of the research. Some clients, however, have clear political, organizational, or personal agendas and will push the researcher to provide results in an unrealistically short time frame or to produce results supporting a particular position. Other times, the subject of the study itself generates controversy; this situation requires the researcher to take extreme care to preserve the neutrality and credibility of the study. Table 2.4 lists a number of strategies that can aid the researcher in planning for sound and credible research (Hedrick, 1986). Several of these strategies attempt to balance client and researcher needs in a responsible fashion, whereas others concentrate on opening the research discussions up to other parties (e.g., advisory groups). In the earliest stages of research planning, it is possible to initiate many of these kinds of activities, thereby bolstering the study's credibility and often its feasibility.

In some instances, the study scope is well-defined by the research sponsors, such as in RFPs and other situations in which a formal statement of work has been developed and worked on prior to contacting the researcher. Even in these instances, however, the researcher typically can provide further fine-tuning of the plan. In other research situations, there is only the vague notion of what the study should address. The following

Table 2.4
Strategies for Credible Research

— *Maintain continuous communication:* Keep all parties aware of the progress of a study and of the efforts that are being made to collect reliable data, to preserve the integrity of the design, and to double-check analysis results. Above all, communicate about progress achieved. Over time, such communication may convince the client of the time requirements for developing reliable data in specific areas.

— *Stay within budget:* The researcher will need to control the costs of the project within the agreed-upon budget. If the researcher believes more funds are needed, then he or she should inform the client as soon as possible. If additional funds are not forthcoming, then the scope of the project will need to be reduced.

— *Negotiate interim products:* When clients insist on results within unrealistic time frames, look for ways to substitute interim products of lesser scope. Perhaps it is impossible to address the effectiveness of a program within 1 year, but it may be possible to provide rich descriptive information on the program's implementation (i.e., ongoing operations or start-up).

— *Form an advisory group:* If constituted appropriately, these groups can be strong assets to studies. The membership should represent all parties relevant to the issue, as well as technical research skills, and the groups should report to the study director rather than the research client. Such a group can be a strong advocate for "doing the job right," and can assist in obtaining the necessary time, cooperation, and resources. They also aid in later dissemination of study results.

— *State study limitations:* From the earliest discussions, it is important to keep the study's limitations in view. Include them in the discussions of study scope, study design, data collection procedures, and results. Keep them visible throughout the life of the study so that the objectivity of the researchers is obvious.

example describes this type of situation and the process that was used to refine the study scope.

Example of Refining the Study Scope

Approximately 7 years ago, a state legislative committee was interested in studying the extent to which mentally ill individuals were living on the streets of the state's cities. The question posed to a state research team in conducting a follow-up review of the deinstitutionalization policies (i.e., policies aimed at reducing the population of the state hospitals) was quite broad: How many homeless people were mentally ill? At this time, homeless individuals on the streets were becoming increasingly visible, particularly on the streets of the state capital. Many of the individuals exhibited symptoms of mental illness. At the same time, the local and national media were printing stories about the homeless postulating that as many as 90% had problems of mental illness and asserting that homelessness might be the product of discharging so many individuals from the state mental health hospitals. Few research studies, however, had yet shed light on the composition of the homeless population.

The task posed to the research team was overwhelming. Little guidance had been provided yet as to how to define homelessness, how best to collect information from individuals on the streets, and how to measure mental illness (through client interviews, history of hospitalizations; exhibits of symptoms, etc.). The task was complicated by the constraints of the legislative research environment—a small research team composed of policy analysts with minimal mental health expertise and with approximately a year to conceptualize, conduct, and report on the study. Given these constraints, the study appeared to be impossible to conduct.

The team, however, began to explore what could be accomplished within these constraints that could shed light on the problem and aid the legislators in assessing state policies and practices regarding deinstitutionalization. Through discussions with members of the legislative committee, the focus of the study was refined to deal with questions concerning the processes used by hospitals to discharge patients and to follow up on clients to determine if they were using community mental health services. In addition to examining questions of hospital practices and procedures, the policy study, using available hospital records and contacts with community mental health centers, examined the question, "How many individuals discharged from state hospitals are still known to the community mental health system?" (or, alternatively, "How many are lost to the system?"). As a subordinate question, the study also attempted to determine how many of these individuals were known to be living on the streets, but it was recognized that this number would not be fully reliable. Furthermore, some persons lost to the community mental health service system could potentially be on the streets as well. The most that could be provided, therefore, was a worst-case estimate of the number of discharged clients who were homeless, based on the unlikely assumption that all discharged individuals who could not be located by the community mental health system were now homeless and living on the streets and in shelters.

Thus although the broad original question was never answered completely, the researchers refocused the study to address much more policy-relevant questions, questions that could be answered more conclusively and whose answers could be used directly to make programmatic changes (see Joint Legislation Audit and Review Commission, 1986; Rog & Henry, 1986).

3

Selecting a Research Design

Stage I of the applied research planning model deals with defining the scope of the research. Having developed at least a preliminary study scope during this stage, the researcher now moves to Stage II, developing a research design and plan. Figure 3.1 provides a reminder of the major activities that occur in Stage II.

During Stage II, the applied researcher needs to perform five activities almost simultaneously—selecting a design, choosing data collection approaches, inventorying resources, assessing the feasibility of executing the proposed approach, and determining trade-offs. These activities and decisions greatly influence each other. Thus preliminary design selections may be revisited after a practical assessment of the resources available to do the study, and data collection plans may be changed after weaknesses in the data sources are discovered during planning. When the dust settles, the end result is a detailed research plan ready for execution. The next four chapters cover the areas noted in Figure 3.1, treating them in sequence, though in reality all may be occurring simultaneously.

The first activity, selecting a research design, is a key decision for research planning, for the design serves as the architectural blueprint of a research project. It ensures that the data collection and analysis activities used to conduct the study are tied adequately to the research questions and that the complete research agenda will be addressed. Selection of a design affects the credibility of the research, its usefulness, and its feasibility. *Credibility* refers to the validity of a study and whether the design is sufficiently sound to provide support for firm conclusions and recommendations. *Usefulness* refers to whether the design is targeted appropriately to answer the specific questions of interest; a sound study is of little use if it answers the wrong questions. *Feasibility* refers to whether the research design and plan are reasonable given the requisite time and other resource constraints. All three factors are important to conducting high-quality applied research. The first two factors are interwoven throughout the next two chapters; the feasibility factor is emphasized in Chapters 5 and 6.

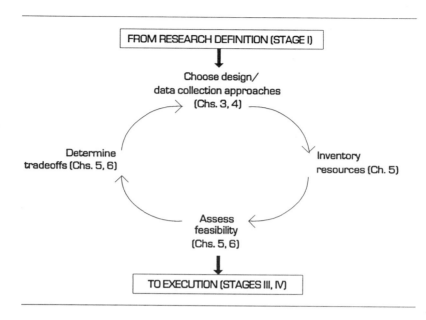

Figure 3.1. Stage II: Development of a Research/Design Plan

MAXIMIZING VALIDITY

A credible research design is one that maximizes validity—it provides a clear explanation of the phenomenon under study and controls all possible biases or confounds that could cloud or distort the research findings. Four types of validity typically are considered when designing applied research (Bickman, 1989; Cook & Campbell, 1979):

Construct validity: the extent to which the constructs in the conceptual framework are operationalized successfully (e.g., measured) in the research study.

Statistical validity: the extent to which the study has used appropriate design and statistical methods to enable it to detect the effects that are present.

Internal validity: this concept applies to impact (cause-effect) questions and refers to the extent to which causal conclusions can be drawn.

External validity: the extent to which it is possible to generalize from the data and context of the research study to broader populations and settings (especially those specified in the statement of the original problem/issue).

All types of validity are important to conducting sound applied research. Their relative emphasis may vary, however, depending on the type of question under study. With impact questions, for example, more emphasis may be placed on internal and statistical conclusion validity than on external validity. Initially, the researcher may be concerned primarily with finding any evidence that a causal relationship exists and be less concerned about the transferability of that effect to other locations. For descriptive questions, external and construct validity may receive greater emphasis. Here the researcher may consider the first priority to be developing a comprehensive and rich picture of a phenomenon; the need to make cause-effect attributions is not relevant.

The concepts of *construct, statistical, internal,* and *external conclusion validity* will appear repeatedly in the next two chapters. Throughout the research planning process, the researcher constantly assesses proposed approaches in terms of their ability to maximize validity.

KEY ITEMS FOR CONSIDERATION

The research design relies heavily on the conceptual framework developed for the study (see Chapter 2). Key information items for design selection are:

- detailed descriptions of the key variables and concepts of interest and how they are expected to be related;
- an outline of the comparisons required to answer the research questions;
- determination of the appropriate level of analysis;
- clarification of population, geographic, and time boundaries; and
- determination of the desired level of precision of the results.

Key Variables and Concepts

The process of refining and revising the research questions in Stage I should have yielded a clear understanding of the key research variables and concepts. For example, if the researcher is charged with determining the extent of high school drug use (a descriptive task), key variables might include drug type, frequency and duration of drug use, drug sales behavior, and so forth. If the study has an impact focus, key variables not only must be identified, but must be specified as independent or dependent variables. Independent variables are the purported causes of change in dependent variables. Again, using the drug use example, if the researcher is to determine whether a recent drug education program led to decreased drug use, the implementation of the drug education program would be specified as the independent variable, and several variables might be posited as potential dependent variables (e.g., frequency of use, type of use).

Attention should be given at this point to reassessing whether the researcher is studying the right variables—that is, whether these are "useful" variables. Unless the researcher is conducting exploratory research to understand better a particular societal problem such as the level of drug use in a city, applied research needs to concentrate on developing information about variables that can be manipulated and changed. If the research is to help inform public policy decisions about remedies, it helps to have reliable information about potentially changeable factors. For example, birth order and birthplace information (unchangeable variables) are much less useful in making policy than information on education or skill training. This does not mean, however, that such variables should be excluded. Variables such as gender, age, or ethnicity can be essential to documenting differential incidence or impacts of phenomena.

Outline of Comparisons

An integral part of design is identifying whether and what comparisons must be made; that is, which variables must be measured and compared with other variables, or with themselves over time. In simple descriptive studies, there are decisions to be made regarding the time frame of an observation and how many observations are appropriate over time. In normative studies, there are further decisions to make concerning what information is appropriate to compare to a standard, and where that standard will be drawn from or how it will be developed. In correlative studies, the design is again an extension of simple descriptive work, with the difference that two or more descriptive measures are arrayed against each other over time to determine if they covary. Impact studies, by far, demand the most judgment and background work. To make the causal attribution that X causes Y, we must be able to compare the condition of Y when X occurred with what the condition of Y *would have been* without X.

Level of Analysis

Knowing what level of analysis is necessary is also critical to answering the "right" question. For example, if we are concerned with high rates of drug use, are we interested in drug use by individual students, aggregate survey totals at the school level, aggregate totals at the school district, or totals for the city as a whole? Do we want to know how many drug sales occurred at a high school, or how many students are selling drugs? Likewise, if we are evaluating a computer training program, do we want to know how many students receiving computer training obtained jobs involving computers after high school, or do we want to know what proportion of high schools report student employment rates greater than 60%?

Correct identification of the proper level of analysis has important implications for how the data will be analyzed. For example, will individual students, schools, or cities be the appropriate level? This issue is discussed further in Chapter 4 in the section dealing with statistical power. The Stage I client discussions aimed at the research questions should have included discussions of appropriate measures. It is likely that the researcher will have to help the client think through the implications of these decisions, providing information about research options and the level of findings that would result. In addition, this is an area that is likely to be revisited if initial data collection plans to obtain data at one level (e.g., the individual student level) prove to be prohibitively expensive. A design fallback position may be to change to an aggregate analysis level (e.g., the school), particularly if data are more readily available and accessible at higher levels of summarization.

Population, Geographic, and Time Boundaries

Population, geographic, and time boundaries are related to external validity issues. Design decisions on these matters affect how generalizable the research results will be—whether the results will be representative of all high school students, all high school students graduating within the past 3 years, all students in urban areas, and so forth. Population and geographic generalizability are probably the most commonly discussed types of generalizability, and researchers frequently have heated debates concerning whether the persons they have studied and the locations where they conducted their study will allow them to address the larger social problem or program of interest.

Time boundaries also can be crucial to the generalizability of the results, especially if the study involves extant data that may be a few years old. With the fast pace of change, it easily can be questioned whether survey data on teenagers just 2 years earlier are reflective of current teens' attitudes and behaviors. Even when decisions are made to collect primary data (new data) for research, attention needs to be paid to specifying the most appropriate time frame (e.g., senior high school students as of fall 1992).

When the researcher cannot study all people, all locations, or all time periods relevant to the problem/program under scrutiny, he or she turns to sampling. Sampling is one of the means by which the researcher "transforms the research questions into a feasible empirical study" (Henry, 1990, p. 14). Sampling allows the researcher to study only a subset of the units of interest and then to generalize to all these units with a specifiable degree of error. It offers benefits in terms of reducing the resources necessary to do a study; it also sometimes permits more intensive scrutiny by allowing a researcher to concentrate attention on fewer cases.

According to Henry (1990), author of *Practical Sampling*, there are only two situations in applied research where sampling may be inadvisable: when the relevant population is very small, and when credibility may be undermined by political considerations. In the first instance, sampling from a small population runs the risk that a single extreme case may influence the outcome disproportionately, or that study consumers may be aware of the omission of a widely known unique case. For example, in research involving the dynamics of homelessness in 20 cities, the diversity of the cities with respect to size, geography, and so forth may prohibit selecting a sample. An example of the second case, when political considerations commonly come into play, involves issues that may have implications for the distribution of public monies. In this instance, inevitably political officials or legislators fail to be persuaded about the generalizability of a study unless it includes their district or city.

Level of Precision

Knowing how precise an answer must be is also crucial to design decisions. The level of desired precision may affect the rigor of the design to be chosen; when sampling is used, the level of desired precision also has important ramifications for how the sample is drawn and the size of samples used. In the initial client discussions, an understanding should be developed as to the precision desired or necessary. Do we care to know only if the drug education program has reduced drug use among high school students and not care about how much? Are we satisfied detecting changes only as large as 20%, or do we want to detect changes as small as 5%? For a computer training program, what are the criteria for success? Is it for students to be 10% more likely to get a job or go on to college, or is it for 50% to do so? Even if program success is a 50% increase, do we care about detecting smaller effects? It is essential to have answers to these kinds of questions during Stage II; if they are not clarified, the research design may later turn out to be inadequate for the client's purposes.

CHOOSING A DESIGN

This book concentrates on three categories of applied research designs: descriptive, experimental, and quasi-experimental. Rather than providing a comprehensive discussion of each of the specific designs, we have chosen to describe major categories of each design, highlighting key features, several of the variations that are possible, the research situations for which each design is most appropriate, and each design's strengths and limitations. We defer discussion of sources and types of data and data collection approaches to Chapter 4, recognizing that there is a wide variety of data collection approaches (e.g., archival records, surveys, behavioral observations, tests) that can be incorporated into these designs.

In our experience, developing an applied research design rarely allows for implementing a design straight from a textbook; rather, the process more typically involves developing hybrids that reflect combinations of designs and other features in an effort to respond to multiple study questions, resource limitations, and other constraints of the research situation (e.g., time deadlines). Thus our intent is to provide the reader with the tools to shape the research approach to the unique aspects of each situation. For those interested in more detailed discussions, several excellent classic sources are available (e.g., Campbell & Stanley, 1966; Cook & Campbell, 1979).

Descriptive Research Designs

Description and Purpose. The overall purpose of descriptive research is to provide a picture of a phenomenon as it naturally occurs, as opposed to studying the impacts of the phenomenon or intervention. Descriptive research can be designed to answer questions of a univariate, normative, or correlative nature (i.e., describing only one variable, comparing the variable to a particular standard, or summarizing the relationship between two or more variables). Thus a descriptive study might assess the prevalence of cocaine use among Missourian 12- to 17-year-olds (purely descriptive question), determine whether knowledge of drugs among this group is sufficient to enable them to pass a test on the topic (normative question), or determine whether there is a relationship between drug use or drug knowledge and age (correlative questions).

A variety of labels are given to descriptive research with different foci. If the longer-term goal of the research is to generate ideas and to embark on a field of inquiry that is relatively unknown, the research often is called *exploratory*. Exploratory research is the least structured form of descriptive research and frequently is used as the first in a series of studies on a specific topic. An example of an exploratory study is a "best practices" study, in which case studies are conducted to document recommended projects in a given program area (e.g., new science education curricula) to learn more about the nature of the program and to identify the lines of inquiry that may be productive to pursue in more focused follow-up studies.

Epidemiologic research is a form of descriptive research that is designed to provide information on the incidence, prevalence, and correlates of a disease or medical condition in a population. Examples of epidemiologic studies include population surveys of the incidence and prevalence of drug use among adults; of the incidence and prevalence of AIDS in specific high-risk populations; and of life-styles, work, and activities associated with specific medical conditions. Attention often is focused on identifying correlates of a disease or condition so that their role as causal agents or mediators may be explored more rigorously in future research.

In the program evaluation arena, practitioners promote several types of descriptive evaluation approaches. The more common designs are process or implementation evaluation reviews (e.g., Scheirer, 1981) and evaluability assessments (Wholey, 1979). In contrast to studying program outcomes, the purpose of process and implementation evaluation is to provide a thorough description of the extent to which a program, policy, or other intervention has been put into place and *how* that has occurred, as well as a description of any barriers that have emerged to thwart the intended implementation plans. Normative comparisons often are made to contrast the "program as implemented" with the "program as intended." Process and implementation evaluations typically are intended to guide the development of a new program and thus are conducted in the early stages of a program.

Evaluability assessment originally was designed as an evaluation planning tool to determine the extent to which an already operating program is ready for an impact evaluation, any changes that are needed to increase its readiness, and the type of evaluation approach most suited to judge the program's performance (Schmidt, Beyna, & Haar, 1982). In order to be considered ready for an evaluation, a program must have well-defined program activities or components, clearly specified goals and effects, and plausible causal linkages between the activities and goals (Rutman, 1980). Thus evaluability assessment can be used to summarize the structure of a program prior to studying its effects. (Note: In practice, however, Rog [1985], in a review of 57 evaluability assessments conducted in the federal government prior to 1984, found that few evaluability assessments led to a subsequent evaluation, regardless of the "evaluation readiness" of the program. It appeared that the descriptive evaluability assessments in some situations provided sufficient information to guide needed program refinements.) Logic modeling techniques, derived from evaluability assessment, also have been used to benefit the development of a program. Rog and Huebner (1992) describe the role of logic modeling and other descriptive evaluation efforts in refining ill-defined interventions during the program development process.

Descriptive approaches are integral parts of addressing normative audit questions or correlative questions. Research questions with words in them such as *compliance, conformance, in accordance with, efficiency, adherence with,* and so on are likely to be normative questions. In this case, descriptive information will need to be developed to compare with a standard, and assessments will have to be made as to whether the current condition (what is or was) meets, exceeds, or falls short of the standard. That standard may be drawn from law, regulations, analyses of legislative intent, professional standards, reasonable judgment, or elsewhere. A conclusion from such an approach might go as follows: "The drinking water in Anywhere County failed to conform to minimum safety standards during 7 of the last 8 tests."

When research questions contain words in them such as *relationship, associated, covariation,* and *related,* it is a clue that these are correlative questions. Again, the design must produce descriptive information, but this time on two or more variables simultaneously so that analyses can be performed to determine whether there is a statistically significant correlation between them. A conclusion from such an approach might go as follows: "Size of dining party and average size of gratuity (tip) were found to be negatively correlated. On a per person basis, larger dining parties were associated with smaller tips, whereas smaller parties were associated with larger tips."

Key Features. Because the category of descriptive research is broad and encompasses a number of different types of designs, one of the easiest ways to distinguish this class of research from others is to identify what it is not; in other words, that *it is not designed to provide information on cause-effect relationships.* Given this distinction, however, there remains a wide range of research alternatives. Unfortunately, other attempts to define the features of descriptive research sometimes have equated it mistakenly with "quick and dirty" studies, or research that is of a less rigorous or systematic nature. Although some descriptive studies are easier to implement than impact studies, the research design process still is guided by an emphasis on maximizing the study's credibility, usefulness, and feasibility. Descriptive studies do not have to be concerned with internal validity, but by their very nature—particularly those that focus on providing information on a specific population or subpopulations—they are more likely to be concerned with maximizing the external validity of the data. Thus unbiased or representative sampling is often a critical design feature.

Even though many descriptive studies are relatively inexpensive as compared to randomized field experiments, others can require considerable resources. Descriptive research that is intended to provide very precise estimates about a population and its subgroups on a number of key variables may be very costly both in terms of money and time, especially if it is necessary to mount large-scale surveys.

Variations. There are only a few features of descriptive research that vary. These features are:

- the representativeness of the study data sources (e.g., the subjects/entities), that is, the manner in which they are selected (e.g., universe, random sample, stratified sample, nonprobability sample);
- the time frame of measurement, that is, whether the study is a one-shot, cross-sectional study or a longitudinal study;
- whether the study involves some basis for comparison (e.g., with a standard, another group or population, data from a previous time period); and
- whether the design is focused on a simple descriptive question, on a normative question, or on a correlative question.

When to Use. Descriptive approaches are appropriate when the researcher is attempting to answer "what is" or "what was" questions, normative questions, or correlative questions. Generally, the information needs are to quantify or characterize some entity or entities in terms of numbers, frequencies, time, cost, or other characteristics. Questions may concern developing a picture of an entity's status, comparing that status to a standard, looking at changes over time, or looking at relationships between variables.

Sometimes descriptive research is only the first effort in a series of research studies on a given subject. It may be the foundation-building activity that allows the researcher better to focus and design future studies of cause-effect relationships. At other times descriptive studies may be used to supplement impact studies, providing a more complete picture of the phenomenon being studied. Examples of three descriptive studies are summarized in Table 3.1.

Strengths. Generally lower costs, relative ease of implementation, and the ability to yield results in a fairly short period of time are strengths of descriptive research, particularly exploratory studies. Yet such research sometimes may require extensive survey resources and intensive measurement efforts. The costs depend on factors such as the size of the sample, the nature of the data sources, and the complexity of the data collection methods employed.

Sometimes, however, the initial projected costs of a study may be deceiving. In the Community Diversion Incentive (CDI) example discussed in Table 3.1, the time frame was tight; results were needed within 6 to 9 months in order to be considered in the next legislative session. Thus it was necessary to conduct the study with extant data. The computerized management information system maintained by the CDI program on participants, as well as the centralized data base maintained by the Department of Corrections on probationers and those incarcerated, were available for the study with rather little difficulty in obtaining access. Upon examination, however, both data sets were woefully inadequate for the study. Much of the data that were critical for the study were missing or considered suspect. Thus both data sets required validation and supplementation with other data sources (e.g., state police records and contacts with CDI local program staff). The time required to review the state police records, maintained on microfiche, and to contact each local CDI program caused a shift in the overall study design; rather than attempt to study all clients in the program, all probationers, and all those incarcerated, samples of each group were selected. Thus the research team redesigned the study to include smaller samples of clients, reducing the overall statistical power of the study but ensuring that information on each individual in the study could be validated and made complete to meet study deadlines.

Table 3.1
Three Examples of Descriptive Studies

Exploratory Research: Developing a Profile of Intensive Case Management

In recent years, case management has become recognized as a critical feature of service delivery to individuals with severe mental illness. Case management provides a mechanism for ensuring that a system of services is responsive to the specific needs of individual clients. In order to provide a more complete understanding of case management practices and policies for severely mentally ill individuals and to identify case management practices that were most appropriate for the homeless among the mentally ill, a review of case management activities was commissioned (Rog, Andranovich, & Rosenblum, 1987). A synthesis was conducted, involving four sources of information: a review of available published and unpublished literature; an examination of selected state efforts; an examination of case management practices in selected local projects; and a series of nominal group processes involving policy, program, and research experts on case management, homelessness, and mental illness. A central finding that emerged from the synthesis was the concept of "intensive case management" for severely mentally ill persons who are homeless or at imminent risk of homelessness. The study led to the development of a profile of intensive case management (e.g., functions, type of case managers, setting, caseload size) that provided the framework for future demonstration program efforts to test the implementation and effectiveness of this form of case management.

Needs Assessment: Using Needs Assessment to Develop a Community's Response to Retail Crime

A detailed needs assessment of the business community in Evanston was conducted for that city's police department through structured in-person interviews with a random sample of 100 retailers (Devitt, Rog, & Bickman, 1981). The survey was the first of its kind to collect actual crime incidence information as well as perceptions of the severity and rate of crime, the quality of service provided by the criminal justice system, and the strategies that can reduce crime. Although shoplifting and check fraud were by far the most common crimes, increased foot patrol was the most desired strategy to reduce crime. In addition, of all police activities, retailers were least satisfied with police efforts in preventing crime. To improve police-retailer relations as well as combat the crime that was experienced, the research team recommended several strategies, including increased foot patrol in certain districts of the city in which the police would visit businesses that were affected by shoplifting and desired an internal security survey. Thus the needs assessment, by including data collection on both actual and perceived needs, provided information that could be used more effectively to combat crime as well as to improve feelings of safety and police-retailer relations.

Program Implementation: Studying the Implementation of a Community Corrections Program

Virginia's Community Diversion Incentive (CDI) program was created by the General Assembly in response to concerns over inmate overcrowding and increasing correctional expenditures (Rog & Henry, 1987). In the fourth year of the project,

(continued)

the General Assembly directed the state's legislative oversight agency to study the program's effectiveness in diverting nonviolent offenders from the state's correctional facilities, thereby presumably reducing costs and the likelihood that nonviolent offenders would become repeat offenders. Because of the program's infancy, the researchers, through discussions with the legislative committee, redirected the focus of the study from the program's impact on recidivism, the correctional population, and operating costs to a focus on the extent to which the program was implemented as designed. That is, although it was too early to conduct a sensitive assessment of the program's impact, it was possible to evaluate a key determinant of the program's implementation—the extent to which the program was serving the intended population of felons who would otherwise have been incarcerated. If the program was not being implemented as intended and was in fact diverting offenders from probation rather than incarceration, it would be unlikely to achieve its intended long-term goals of reducing prison overcrowding and correction expenditures.

In contrast to more common implementation studies, the CDI evaluation used a unique application of a statistical technique, logit analysis, to focus on the extent to which the target population was being served. The technique led to quantifiable results that easily were summarized and communicated to policymakers. Furthermore, quantitative descriptive results could be used to calculate the program's potential short-term cost savings for consideration by policymakers. Because the program had indeed produced an immediate cost savings and appeared to be at least partially fulfilling its promise, the program was continued, and a more comprehensive impact evaluation was slated once the program was deemed sufficiently mature.

In many cases, results from descriptive research designs are relatively straightforward to analyze and to communicate effectively to a range of audiences. Survey results, for example, often involve the computation of simple population estimates (e.g., the percentage of local high school students currently using drugs) that can be understood by individuals with minimal understanding of research. Because much descriptive research is done with emphasis on defining and representing the characteristics of specific populations, it is often strong on external validity (e.g., epidemiologic research).

Limitations. Descriptive research is not intended to answer questions of a causal nature. Major problems can arise when the results from descriptive studies are used inappropriately to make causal inferences, a temptation for consumers of correlational data. The story is told often in statistics classes that a state legislator once observed that based on his analysis of the relationship between teachers' salaries and alcohol sales in the state, he could not in good conscience recommend salary raises. "All you have to do is look at the data for previous years," he is reported to have said. "As teachers' pay increased, so did alcohol sales;

if we pay them more, they'll drink more." He interpreted a positive correlation between teachers' salaries and state alcohol consumption as causal, ignoring the many other explanatory possibilities and even the differences in units of analysis (teachers vs. all state residents).

Researchers can help prevent the misutilization of descriptive data by emphasizing the limits of the designs and by stating clearly what can and cannot be concluded. The general public is becoming increasingly more familiar with descriptive data as a function of media surveys, consumer marketing studies, and opinion polls, as are print, radio, and television reporters. Although the increased amount of descriptive data creates more opportunities for misuse (e.g., the oat bran and cholesterol research), the increased sophistication of the research consumer and the media work in the opposite direction.

Experimental Research Designs

Description and Purpose. The primary purpose in conducting an experimental study is to test the existence of a causal relationship among two or more variables. In an experimental study, one variable, the independent variable, is varied or manipulated systematically so that its effects on another variable, the dependent variable, can be measured.

In applied social research, the independent variable may be a treatment or a specific program; the conditions of the independent variable are typically whether individuals or entities did or did not participate in a treatment or program. In a study to test the effects of a health education curriculum on students' general health attitudes and behaviors, for example, students could be assigned randomly to either one of two levels of the treatment variable: the treatment group, which would receive instruction according to the new curriculum, or the control group, which would not receive any health instruction. The differences between the subsequently measured attitudes and behavior of the treatment and control groups form the basis of estimating the program effects.

Key Features. The distinguishing characteristic of an experimental study is the random assignment of individuals or entities to the levels or conditions of the study. Random assignment is used to control all biases at the time of assignment and to ensure that only one variable— the independent (experimental) variable—differs between conditions. Through random assignment, all individuals have an equal likelihood of being assigned to either the treatment group or the control group. If the total number of individuals or entities assigned to treatment and control groups is sufficiently large, then any differences between the groups should be small and attributable to chance.

The emphasis in an experimental study is on maximizing internal validity by controlling possible confounding variables. Thus, in the study of the effects of a health education curriculum, children in both the treatment and control conditions should be of similar age and educational attainment to control for any differential previous education in health or related subjects, as well as any differences in cognitive development. In order to institute random assignment procedures and maximum control of the research context, researchers often stress internal validity, sometimes limiting the scope of the study (e.g., examining only those individuals who are willing to participate in a randomized experiment) even if doing so limits the study's external validity (generalizability).

Variations. To describe the various types of designs, we have adopted the notational system developed by Campbell and Stanley (1966) and widely used by others. In this system, X stands for a "treatment" or the independent variable; O stands for an observational measurement of the dependent variable; and R indicates that the groups involved were formed by random assignment of individuals from the same population. Subscripts 1 through n refer to the treatment number or observation number when more than one treatment or observation is involved.

The most basic experimental study is called a *post only* design, in which individuals are assigned randomly to either a treatment or control group and the measurement of the effects of the treatment is conducted at a time period following the administration of the treatment. The design notation is as follows:

| Group 1 | R | X | O |
| Group 2 (control) | R | | O |

There are a number of variations to this simple experimental design that can respond to specific information needs, as well as provide control over possible confounds or influences that may exist. Among the features that can be varied are the following:

- The number and scheduling of posttest measurement or observation periods. In a study of the effects of the health education curriculum, for example, it may be of interest to study children's knowledge immediately following the class to assess initial comprehension, and 3 months after the curriculum is complete to assess longer-term knowledge retention. Thus this design would look as follows:

Group 1	R	X	O1	O2
Group 2	R		O1	O2

Note that the researcher using this design must rely heavily on the randomization process to yield equivalent groups with respect to prior knowledge levels. Thus if the randomization process should fail, the researcher will have no information about the equivalence of the groups before randomization. Although more expensive, pretest measures are desirable whenever possible.

- Whether a preliminary observation (or "preobservation") is conducted. For example, there may be an interest in assessing changes in knowledge from before and after the curriculum was introduced. This design is called a *pre-post* design and looks as follows:

Group 1	R	O1	X	O2
Group 2	R	O1		O2

- The number of treatment and control groups used. In some research situations, there is a need to study systematically several levels of treatment. For example, there may be a need to compare three different types of health education curricula (X1, X2, X3) upon children's knowledge as follows:

Group 1	R	O1	X1	O2
Group 2	R	O1	X2	O2
Group 3	R	O1	X3	O2
Group 4	R	O1		O2

It is even possible to add another randomized control group when the researcher desires to know the extent to which a pretest itself has had an effect on posttest scores (independent of X). This is known as the *Solomon Four-Group Design*.

Group 1	R	O1	X	O2
Group 2	R	O1		O2
Group 3	R		X	O2
Group 4	R			O2

Table 3.2

Two Examples of Randomized Studies

Program Impact: Assessing the Impact of a Work Registration Requirement for Welfare Recipients

The Food and Nutrition Service of the U.S. Department of Agriculture mounted a study to determine the effectiveness of a work requirement for recipients of food stamps. Under new legislation, all able-bodied unemployed food stamp recipients were expected to register for work at local employment service offices. In order to determine the effectiveness of this requirement in speeding the movement of persons capable of working off the welfare rolls, a randomized evaluation was mounted to determine the impact of the requirement. Food stamp recipients were assigned randomly to either the treatment group (subject to the work registration requirement) or the control group (not subject to the work registration requirement). It was necessary for sites to obtain waivers to exempt control group members from the work registration requirement. This aspect of a much larger study can be categorized as a posttest-only randomized experiment, with emphasis on subsequent welfare receipt and earnings. Although much demographic and employment history information could be gathered for each individual, the very fact that the target group was unemployed at the time of the intervention made past information regarding employment history generally useful only for refining the analysis rather than supporting a pre-post comparison.

Program Impact: Do Financial Incentives Improve School Academic Performance?

In an attempt to learn if financial incentives for encouraging and rewarding improvements in school academic performance affect achievement, researchers at the Vanderbilt Institute for Public Policy worked with Tennessee education officials to develop the School Studies Improvement Incentives Project (Bickman, 1985). In this project, school performance, rather than teacher performance, was measured and was compared against the school's own past performance to determine if the school was to receive an award. No specific improvement program was imposed on the schools, and the schools made their own decisions on how to use funds they were awarded.

A critical aspect of the design of this evaluation was that *schools,* not students or classes, were the unit of analysis. Thus the researchers had to recruit a sufficient number of schools to participate in the study. The commissioner of education met with school superintendents throughout the state in order to persuade them to participate. Of the 147 school systems in the state, 36 indicated interest in participating in the study, representing a pool of 270 elementary schools. After telephone calls and site visits, the number of schools was reduced to the targeted 100 schools. The study was designed as a randomized experiment with schools randomly assigned to either the program (which was simply a reward program) or a control group (which received additional testing but was not eligible for the financial rewards).

Relevant to this discussion is how the principals perceived the randomization procedures. Although the research team visited all the principals and produced attractive information brochures about the project with full explanations of the randomization process, it was still felt necessary to gauge the principals' understanding of the project. Two specific questions were asked about the randomization process: (a) Will all participating schools have an even chance of being selected to be in the incentive group, and (b) is there a way that you can enhance your school's chance of being selected into the incentive group next year? Eighty-six percent got question 1 right, 70% answered question 2 correctly, and only 60% of the principals got both questions correct. Regardless of the project's efforts to inform and educate the principals about the randomization procedure, a significant percentage of them still did not fully understand the randomization process. Clearly, researchers need to be extremely diligent with research participants.

As noted throughout this text, conducting studies in the real world will predictably produce unpredictable events that will affect the design of the study. After the schools agreed to participate, but before random assignment, the state passed legislation that forbid the use of any state funds to implement or study financial incentives in schools. This legislation was not aimed at this project in particular, but at the governor's career ladder program. This caused a delay of 1 year in implementing the study. During that time, new school superintendents were elected, schools closed, and principals were replaced. Attrition was responsible for a loss of 13 schools. Thus it was important to obtain new formal agreements with officials before random assignment was conducted. In this way, dropouts occurred from the group as a whole rather than differential attrition from control and treatment groups. The benefits of waiting until the last possible moment to conduct random assignment should be clear.

The results of the first year of implementation did not show any significant effects of the financial incentives on academic achievement. Thus it was decided to offer half the schools a technical assistance package that would help them implement a school improvement program. This part of the study was also conducted as a randomized experiment with half the schools eligible for the incentives and half in the incentive control group randomly assigned to the technical assistance group, and the other half receiving no technical assistance. All of the incentive schools and 86% of the control group schools continued to participate. The results of the second year of implementation were only slightly more encouraging. The added technical assistance did not produce any impact on achievement, either alone or in combination with financial incentives. Data indicated that incentive eligible schools where teachers had positive attitudes toward the incentive program had significantly increased their academic achievement. Attitudes had no role in determining academic achievement in the control schools. Even though these results were statistically significant, they were not of such a nature to recommend that the incentive program should be adopted as a policy for the state even though state education officials thought highly of the intervention.

Table 3.2 illustrates two different types of experimental designs in applied contexts.

When to Use. An experimental study is the most appropriate approach to select when studying cause-effect relationships. There are certain situations that are especially conducive for randomized experiments (Cook & Campbell, 1979):

- When random assignment is expected. For example, admissions to magnet schools often are expected to be on a random basis from a selected pool of eligible student applicants.
- When demand outstrips supply for an intervention. For example, suppose there are more applicants for the health education program than can possibly be served. Absent other information, the fairest decision rule is random selection.
- When there are multiple entry groups over a period of time—that is, all individuals will receive services eventually, but within the first few months, only a fixed number can be served.

Nevertheless, in applied settings, random assignment of individuals to treatment and control conditions is not easy to undertake. Program operators can be very reluctant to deny services to members of a control group, even on a temporary basis, and even when the program is already at capacity and there is no evidence of its effectiveness. Assigning individuals to a control group means that they must not enter the treatment as long as data are being collected. For many longitudinal studies, this may be a number of years. During this time, an individual in the control group may get "worse" and appear to need the services the treatment group is receiving. Although the treatment has not been demonstrated to be effective, it usually has more resources. This factor can lead practitioners not to favor random assignment. Further constraints come from the fact that applied researchers often are asked to undertake studies of program impacts only after the program is already ongoing, when it is often too late to use random assignment. Design options for situations where random assignment is not feasible to implement are discussed in the next section on quasi-experiments.

Strengths. The overwhelming strength of a randomized experiment is its control over threats to internal validity (i.e., its ability to rule out potential alternative explanations for apparent treatment or program effects). This is a major strength in design and is not to be taken lightly. The same strength, however, also can operate as a weakness. As noted earlier, the more controlled and sterile an intervention or program becomes (the more it resembles a controlled special study), and the less it resembles the usual real-world intervention, the less likely it is that its findings will be applicable to a wide range of settings, populations, and time periods.

Limitations. Randomized experiments can be difficult to implement with integrity, particularly in settings where the individuals responsible for random assignment procedures lack research training or understanding of the importance of maintaining compliance with the research protocol (Bickman, 1985; Cochran, 1978). The integrity of the design may be challenged, for example, if program operators or others begin to perceive positive effects of an intervention and "waive" the rules for certain individuals. Yet even in these circumstances, in-depth staff training, centralization of randomization procedures, or rigorous monitoring procedures can help maintain the design's integrity.

The integrity of the design also may be challenged by differential attrition from the groups, typically by more individuals dropping out of the control condition. The result of the attrition could result in a nonequivalent control group comprising only a subset of those initially assigned to the program, as well as a group too small in number to provide the statistical power necessary to detect the expected effects of the intervention. In certain types of studies, attrition can be anticipated, and strategies can be built into the process either to prevent or to control the effects of attrition. These strategies can include offering control group participants some incentive for remaining in the group (e.g., payment for participation in data collection efforts); providing some alternative treatment (e.g., status quo treatment) rather than no treatment at all; employing more rigorous and extensive tracking procedures, particularly in longitudinal studies in which attrition is expected to grow over the course of the study; and selecting a larger number of control participants than needed based on expected rates of attrition. Clearly, all of these strategies involve trade-offs and must be considered in light of the resources available.

There are problems in implementing experimental studies even when the situation appears particularly conducive to randomization. For example, in conducting research involving homeless individuals, there are instances in which the most equitable distribution of scarce resources, such as housing and services, is allocation on a randomized basis (e.g., through a lottery). Although this type of distribution often is accepted by service providers and advocates, they may be opposed to attempts to take advantage of this randomization process for research purposes. The advocacy community also may be inclined to protect unsuccessful lottery participants from further scrutiny and data collection (i.e., as part of a control group), feeling that it violates the privacy of a vulnerable group. To counteract these problems, the researcher must spend effort to understand the overall context and all parties' views regarding the research, to develop research strategies that are minimal in burden and that compensate participants for their time, and to communicate the research agenda to all interested parties so as to prevent misinterpretations of the goals and ultimate uses of the research. Without these additional efforts, it is likely that the study either will not be mounted or will be challenged throughout its implementation; at worst, the researcher who proceeds without the full support and "buy-in" of all interested parties (particularly in sensitive research areas) may find himself or herself on a blacklist of service providers that ultimately can block any future research efforts in that community.

Finally, experimental studies typically are considered the "creme de la research enterprise," and are viewed as the necessary design for funding by federal research agencies. The emphasis on experimentation can result, at times, in research on relatively less important (even trivial) questions that are more readily conducive to random assignment. In essence, the situation can be one in which the opportunity for random assignment drives the question to be addressed, rather than the reverse.

Quasi-Experimental Designs

Description and Purpose. Quasi-experimental designs have the same primary purpose as experimental studies: to test the existence of a causal relationship among two or more variables. They are the design of necessity when random assignment is impossible. Like experiments, quasi-experiments' abilities to estimate program or treatment impacts depend on being able to establish a comparison base, in this case a nonrandomized comparison base appropriate for contrasting with the treatment group to estimate impact.

Key Features. Quasi-experiments attempt to approximate the true experiment by substituting other design features for the randomization process. There are generally two ways to create a quasi-experimental comparison base: by the addition of nonequivalent comparison groups or by the addition of pre- and post-treatment observations on the treated group (or preferably both).

If comparison groups are used, they generally are referred to as nonequivalent groups; they cannot be exactly equivalent with the treatment group because they were not formed by random assignment. The researcher, however, strives to develop procedures to make these groups as equivalent as possible, thereby providing a reasonable basis for using them to contrast with the treated group to estimate impact. The comparison group and preobservation features of quasi-experimental designs are intended to provide necessary information and control to enable researchers to rule out competing explanations for their results.

Variations. Quasi-experiments vary along several of the same dimensions that are relevant for experiments. Table 3.3 lists a number of possible designs that frequently are described in research methods texts. Note that the R for randomization is absent and that no groups are designated as "control" groups, a term reserved for a randomized no-treatment group in true experiments. In many applied research situations, however, the design selected will reflect some combination of the textbook designs, especially when the researcher is tasked with answering multiple kinds of questions.

Overall there are two main types of quasi-experiments: those involving data collection from two or more nonequivalent groups, and those involving taking multiple observations over time. Quasi-experimental designs can vary along the following dimensions:

- the number and scheduling of postmeasurement or postobservation periods,
- the number and scheduling of premeasurement or preobservation periods,
- the nature of the observations (i.e., whether the preobservation uses the same measurement procedure as the postobservation, or whether both are using measures that are proxies for the real concept),
- the manner in which the treatment and comparison groups are determined, and
- whether the treatment group serves as its own comparison group or one or more separate comparison groups are used.

Nonequivalent group designs are based on creating comparison groups for the treatment group by using selection criteria to substitute for random assignment. Examples of procedures for creating such a group include using members of a waiting list for a program/service; using people who did not volunteer for a program, but were eligible; using students in classes that will receive the curriculum (treatment) at a later date; and matching individual characteristics.

Interrupted time-series designs are marked by multiple observations, both before and after an intervention or treatment is introduced. Examples of the results of two time-series designs are illustrated in Figure 3.2. The purpose of a time-series design is to detect changes in the data trends before and after the intervention that can be attributed to the intervention itself. Generally, analysts look for changes in slope or level of a series concurrent with onset of an intervention; Example A in

Table 3.3

Quasi-Experimental Designs

Nonequivalent Comparison Group: Post Only

Group 1	X	O1	
Group 2		O2	

Nonequivalent Comparison Group: Pre-Post

Group 1	O1	X	O2
Group 2	O1		O2

Nonequivalent Comparison Group: Multiple Treatments, Pre-Post

Group 1	O1	X1	O2
Group 2	O1	X2	O2
Group 3	O1	X3	O2
Group 4	O1		O2

Interrupted Time Series: Simple

O1	O2	O3	O4	O5	X	O6	O7	O8	O9	O10	O11

Interrupted Time Series: With Comparison Series

O1	O2	O3	O4	O5	X	O6	O7	O8	O9	O10	O11
O1	O2	O3	O4	O5		O6	O7	O8	O9	O10	O11

Interrupted Time Series: With Onset (X) and Offset (−X) of Treatment

O1	O2	O3	O4	X	O5	O6	O7	−X	O8	O9	O10

Example A

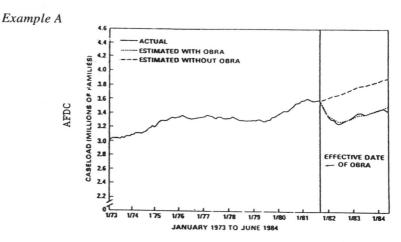

Example B

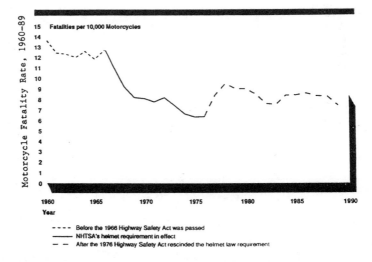

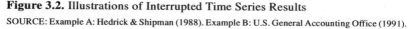

Figure 3.2. Illustrations of Interrupted Time Series Results
SOURCE: Example A: Hedrick & Shipman (1988). Example B: U.S. General Accounting Office (1991).

Figure 3.2 shows a simple interrupted time-series design that was used by the U.S. General Accounting Office (1984b) when studying the impact of tightening AFDC program eligibility requirements on monthly caseloads.

Some of the strongest time-series designs supplement a time series for the treatment group with comparison time series for another group (or time period). Another powerful variation occurs when the researcher is able to study the effects of an intervention over time under circumstances where that intervention is initiated and later withdrawn. Example B shows such a design as applied to assessing the impact of the 1966 Highway Safety Act requiring motorcycle riders to wear helmets (GAO, 1991). As increasing numbers of states passed such laws, fatalities declined; when states began to repeal helmet laws, fatalities increased. The time-series design showing changes in both level and slope of the series concurrent with the onset and offset of the intervention (helmet laws) is powerful both analytically and visually.

When to Use. A quasi-experimental design is not the method of choice, but rather a fallback strategy for situations in which random assignment is not possible. Situations such as these include:

- when the nature of the independent variable precludes using random assignment (e.g., exposure or involvement in a natural disaster);
- retrospective studies (e.g., the program is already over or well under way);
- studies focused on economic or social conditions (e.g., unemployment);
- when randomization is too expensive, not feasible to initiate, or impossible to monitor closely;
- when there are obstacles to withholding the treatment or when it seems unethical to withhold it; and
- when the timeline is tight, and a quick decision is mandated.

As noted earlier, a quasi experiment also can become the default design when random assignment breaks down during the implementation of a project or if there is considerable attrition from either the treatment or control group, thus creating nonequivalent groups.

Strengths. The major strength of the quasi-experimental design is that it provides an approximation to the experimental design and that, with care, it can support causal inferences. Although often open to various types of threats to internal validity, the quasi experiment does provide a mechanism for chipping away at the uncertainty surrounding the existence of a specific causal relationship. Additional nonequivalent comparison groups also can bolster an experimental design, particularly if it is focused narrowly.

A good example of how such designs can be used to make incremental progress in understanding a societal problem is in the area of teenage pregnancy. Previous research had indicated that teenage pregnancy had significant effects on girls in terms of later income, educational achievement, and welfare status—putting them on the economic slow track. It generally is accepted, however, that teenage pregnancy is more likely to be found among children of economically disadvantaged families, a potentially confounding factor.

Obviously, in our quest to estimate the effect of teenage pregnancy on later life circumstances, we would not randomly assign teenage girls to become or not to become pregnant. According to Blinder (1991), though, Geronimus and Korenman developed an innovative quasi-experimental strategy of using as a nonequivalent comparison group the sisters of girls who became pregnant in their teens, but who themselves delayed childbirth to at least age 20. This comparison group allowed the researcher to have some measure of control for family economic disadvantage variables. When this comparison base was used, initial results indicate that the previously found negative outcomes associated with teenage pregnancy were reduced significantly in terms of income, and essentially disappeared with respect to education (completion of high school) and welfare use. There are a number of other questions that immediately come to mind about the equivalence of the comparison groups in this research; however, it shows the creative use of a new comparison base for studying a widely researched problem.

In many instances, quasi-experimental designs have an advantage over randomized experiments of being relatively easy for the nontechnical research client or consumer to understand. This is especially true for interrupted time-series designs when the graphic plots of observations visually convey the same results as the statistical analysis.

Limitations. The greatest vulnerability to quasi-experimental designs is the possibility that the comparison base created is biased, that it does not give an accurate estimate of what the situation would have been in the absence of the treatment or program. For example, suppose that a quasi-experimental design is composed of two groups: a treatment group consisting of the first students to complete a health education program, and a comparison group consisting of the students on the waiting list for the program. To estimate the program's impact, the researcher compares both groups' knowledge of healthy eating habits after the first group has completed the program. In making this comparison to estimate impact, the researcher is making the assumption that he or she has controlled for any motivational differences between the groups by using only students who obviously are interested in the educational topic— they either enrolled in the program or were on the waiting list.

Nevertheless, are motivational differences controlled? What if the first students to take the program were also the first to register for it (i.e., a first-come, first-served enrollment procedure)? If so, then there may be a potentially confounding factor in that those registering quickest were more motivated than those registering later, and therefore they may have entered the program with greater knowledge. In this case, the research design would be biased toward making the program look better than it actually is as a result of preexisting differences in health knowledge between the two groups.

A similar example might be found in a remedial training program designed for the unemployed. The earliest volunteers for the training services may be the most motivated because they have the most immediate need. They have further to progress before being ready for employment. In this case the bias might operate in the opposite direction, making the program look less effective than it actually is.

To some degree, these kinds of problems can be minimized if one or more preintervention observations are taken on both groups, especially pretest measures on any variables that are believed to be predictive of the dependent variable of interest. Statistical adjustments can then be made to control at least partially for any group nonequivalencies on measured factors. Unfortunately, if the groups differ on unknown factors or unmeasurable factors, the analytic correction will be flawed. Nevertheless, it is always in the researcher's best interest to explore the possibility of confounds, to understand them as thoroughly as possible, and to make any appropriate analytic adjustments. Throughout both the planning and execution phases of an applied research project, researchers must keep their eyes open to identify potential rival explanations for their results.

Interrupted time-series designs have the disadvantage of sometimes being difficult to interpret. The timing of the treatment or interruption is not always clear or definitive; in fact, it is usually advisable to collect descriptive data on the timing and diffusion of the intervention prior to analyzing time-series data. An example would be collecting information about localities' degree of enforcement of a new seat belt law prior to analyzing the law's effects on numbers of state traffic injuries or fatalities. In such a case, if it were found that there were substantial differences in whether localities were enforcing the new law, the analyst would want to supplement the statewide analysis with grouped analyses to determine if localities that are enforcing the law show more of an impact than those not enforcing it. Separate time series might be plotted for each locality to illustrate such patterns visually.

Another limitation on interrupted time-series designs is the some-times extensive data requirements for multiple observations across time, a limitation regarding their applicability in contexts where the researcher does not have access to extant data and must rely on primary data collection. Even when archival data exist, they must be evaluated carefully for both data quality and relevance decisions (see Chapter 4).

"NOT SO OBVIOUS" MISTAKES IN DESIGN: LEARNING FROM PAST EXPERIENCES

As discussed in the preface, one of our purposes of writing a book on applied research design is to offer lessons from both our mistakes and successes that can inform students and other practitioners. We offer two examples of not-so-obvious mistakes from research we have conducted that have improved our planning of subsequent studies.

Example 1: Understanding the "Black Box" Before Designing the Study

As discussed throughout Chapters 1 and 2, gaining a thorough under-standing of the problem or issue under study is a key aspect of planning an applied research study. Although this advice appears to be quite natural and commonsensical, the depth of what you need to know in the beginning may not always be apparent.

Having received federal funding to conduct a modest evaluation of its juvenile diversion program for status offenders, a county juvenile court commissioned an evaluation of the effectiveness of the program in reducing recidivism. (A status offense refers to a juvenile engaging in a behavior, such as running away from home, that would not be an offense if engaged in by an adult.) Several discussions ensued between the re-searchers and the program funders. Much of the discussion focused on the nature and goals of the program, desired measures, data quality and availability, and the types of comparison that were available. Status quo treatment (involving the normal court and probation procedures) was viewed as the most logical basis of comparison with the new program.

Furthermore, through discussions, it was learned that children who are status offenders enter the court through three different avenues: walk-ins (with their parents), police referrals, and mail-ins (children identified by police but not detained). Although all were considered important, the mail-in referrals were most amenable to random assignment. It was possible for the researchers to prepare an a priori random assignment procedure that would allow for group determination as soon as a mail-in referral was received. Random assignment of the walk-in and police referrals was not considered possible, as it would involve someone at the program to detour individuals physically from the program to the court if they were randomly assigned to the control group. This procedure was considered to be too confusing and open to corruption; thus it was decided to assign randomly only the mail-in referrals.

The study was conducted over the course of 12 months. Data were monitored, and the integrity of the random assignment procedure was checked routinely. All data on individuals in both groups were reviewed painstakingly, validated, and supplemented with manual file data. A number of analyses were conducted, yielding no difference on all dependent measures. Careful in-depth reviews were conducted, with no further explanation than that the diversion treatment had no measurable short-term impact on the juveniles. When the results were reviewed with the research sponsor, the comment was, "No difference? That doesn't surprise me; I wouldn't expect a difference." After we picked ourselves up off the floor, we learned that because the majority of mail-in referrals were typically curfew violators, the program treatment and the control or status quo treatment were essentially the same: a figurative slap on the hand and some family counseling. Therefore our study had essentially studied two similar treatments! The lesson learned was to study the intervention of the control group as well as the treatment group; knowing the experiences of control and comparison groups is as important as knowing what ensues in the treatment group.

**Example 2: Knowing the Focus
of Your Study**

Another not-so-obvious design mistake can occur with the targeting of the program itself. In line with its concerns for employee health and well-being, a Fortune 500 corporation initiated a multiphase health improvement and stress management program for middle managers and their spouses and commissioned an evaluation of its outcomes. The evaluation involved a pretest-posttest nonequivalent group design, with both program and comparison group participants receiving questionnaires 1 month prior and 6 months following the workshops. Program participation, however, did not appear to have any effects on the health status of either managers or their spouses.

Further internal analyses of open-ended questions into the nature of the stress affecting the managers revealed that the nature of the job stress experienced (i.e., organization stress) differed from the type of stress for which the program was targeted. Therefore the program's emphasis on personal coping strategies may not have been appropriate for the communication problems the managers were confronting. Although the internal analyses of these problems (i.e., the feedback research approach; Rog & Bickman, 1984) increased the utility of the overall evaluation, the intervention was not given an appropriate test. More in-depth understanding of the preexisting stress problem and the logic of the program beforehand could have helped in guiding programming decisions during the development stage (either by targeting the program to the appropriate population or redesigning the program to fit the needs of the target population).

CONTRASTING FEATURES OF APPLIED AND BASIC DESIGN

As we have seen, the differences between applied and basic research have substantial implications for potential design choices. In Chapter 1, numerous contrasts were made regarding the purpose, contexts, and methods of applied research. Applied research, for example, is much more likely than basic research to be problem oriented and to be concerned with answering multiple questions by discovering "practically significant" results. Applied research is more likely to be conducted in the field or to be initiated after the treatment or program has begun, thus forcing the researcher to rely on quasi-experimental methods. Applied research is more likely to place greater emphasis on external validity (generalizability of results), to settle for less precision, and to employ multiple methods and multiple levels of analysis.

The next chapter highlights differences in the types of data usually collected by applied and basic researchers. Data sources for applied researchers are more likely to include administrative records, and there is a greater emphasis on using "real" outcome measures. In sum, the messy and complex research context of the real world drives the applied researcher to use more complex methodologies, substituting multiple methods and convergent analyses for the control basic researchers are able to exert in the laboratory.

4

Selecting Data Collection Approaches

Concurrent with the design decisions of Chapter 3, the researcher is investigating possible data collection approaches (see Figure 4.1). These activities are actually inseparable, as choices made regarding design and data collection procedures must be congruent. Studies, particularly those investigating multiple research questions, often encompass several data collection efforts. This chapter begins with a discussion of the data collection issues that must be considered during the planning stage, including the sources of data available, the form in which the data are available, the amount of data needed, the accuracy and reliability of the data, and whether the data fit the parameters of the design. The chapter then reviews the major methods of data collection that are used in applied research and discusses the need for an analysis plan. Examples of analysis plans also are included.

DATA COLLECTION CONSIDERATIONS

In considering data collection approaches, the researcher is seeking to find an economical but accurate way to obtain data to fit the conceptual framework underlying the study. At the start, several questions are posed:

- What are the likely sources of the data?
- In what form are the data?
- Will there be a sufficient amount of data?
- How accurate and reliable are the data?
- How well do the data fit the potential study design?

Sources of Data

The researcher should identify the likely sources of data to address the research questions. Data often are described in one of two broad categories: primary data and secondary data. Among the potential primary data sources that exist for the applied researcher are people (e.g., community leaders, program participants, service providers, the

68

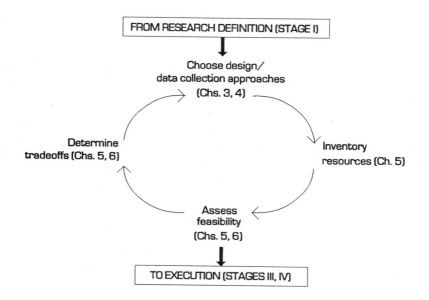

Figure 4.1. Stage II: Development of a Research/Design Plan

general public); independent descriptive observations of events, activities, and so forth; physical documents; and test results. Secondary sources can include administrative records, economic and social indicators, prior research studies, fugitive unpublished research literature, and secondary or archival data sets. Given a sound literature review in Stage I and discussions with current experts in the substantive area, researchers generally should have sufficient knowledge of the potential data sources very early in the planning process. If the research topic is a relatively new one, it may quickly become obvious that the planned research will not be able to rely upon or use existing data and will need to engage in primary data collection.

Form of the Data

The form in which the data are found is a very important factor for any applied research project and may even determine the overall feasibility of the study. Some projects are easy to conduct; the data sources are obvious, and the data already are gathered, archived, and computerized. It is then only a matter of requesting access and transferring files. Other projects are extremely difficult; identifying the appropriate sources for the needed information may be confusing, and it may turn out that the procedures necessary for obtaining the information are expensive and time-consuming. It may sometimes be so difficult that the study is not feasible—at least not within the available level of resources.

Possible forms of data include:

- self-reports (e.g., attitudes, opinions, memories, characteristics, and circumstances of individuals),
- computerized or manual (i.e., hard-copy) research data bases or administrative records,
- observations (i.e., events, actions, or circumstances that need to be described or recorded), and
- various kinds of documentary evidence (e.g., letters, invoices, receipts, meeting minutes, memoranda, plans, reports).

Self-Report Data

When dealing with self-reported data, the researcher may ask the individual research participant to provide, to the best of his or her ability, information on the areas of interest. These inquiries may be made through individual interviews, through telephone or mail surveys, or through written corroboration or affirmation.

Extant Data

When dealing with extant data from archival sources, the researcher generally is using the data for a purpose other than that for which they were collected originally. Professional norms are changing slowly to encourage (and in some cases to require) researchers to make their data available to others for purposes of reanalysis or new work (see Boruch & Cordray, 1985; Committee on National Statistics, 1985). There are a number of secondary data sources, such as those developed by university consortia, federal sources such as the Bureau of the Census, and commercial data sources such as *Inform* (a data base of 550 business journals). Federal research funders and journal editors increasingly are requiring grant and contract recipients and authors to release data to others who have legitimate research inquiries under way. This pressure is the result of both the reality of tight funding for applied research and a greater professional awareness of the potential benefits available from establishing science archives. Nevertheless, there can be substantial hurdles regarding data access and release, especially when safeguards need to be instituted to protect the confidentiality of the original research participants.

Administrative data pose other issues. Given the enormous amount of information collected on individuals in American society, administrative data bases are a potential bonanza for applied researchers. More and more programs, for example, are computerizing their administrative data and archiving the full data base at least monthly. Management information systems, in particular, are becoming more common in service settings for programmatic and evaluation purposes as well as for financial disbursement purposes.

Administrative data sets, however, have one drawback in common with data bases for past research: They were constructed originally for operational purposes, not to meet the specific objectives of the researcher's task. Thus variables on the data set may be only approximations to the variables employed in a study's conceptual framework; the values of variables may not be coded optimally; and the update procedures for the files may periodically write over information on an individual as their status changes, thus eliminating the researcher's ability to study changes. As with research data bases, extensive precautions need to be followed to avoid disclosing identities of individuals included in the administrative files.

Two previously described studies provide examples of the types of difficulties that can be encountered in using administrative records. In the deinstitutionalization study discussed earlier, one of the data bases examined was maintained by the state hospital system for financial reimbursement purposes. Although the data base appeared to contain much information that was useful to the study in tracking individuals following discharge from the hospitals, upon inspection it was discovered that only the data pertinent to reimbursement issues were complete and validated. Discharge status, for example, was typically listed as "discharged to self" even if the individual was being discharged to family, to a board and care home, and so forth.

In the GAO study of effects of AFDC eligibility tightening, the researchers found it necessary to devote a single analyst full-time to each of the two research sites where state computerized welfare files were the major data source. This was because it was necessary to link monthly computerized records to create 13-month longitudinal records for each individual, and to do so required becoming intimately familiar with each state's record-keeping management information systems (Hedrick & Shipman, 1988). In the planning stage of the same study, one site was dropped during pilot testing because creating the required 13-month longitudinal welfare participation record would have necessitated going to three separate data sources (i.e., microfiche, microfilm, and manual file record) for each month (13 times) for each of the several hundred individuals being studied.

The checklist in Table 4.1, drawn from Rog and Landis (1985), may be helpful to the researcher in evaluating the quality and utility of secondary data, especially when the data are to be drawn from administrative data bases. Questions that need to be asked include the following:

- Are the records complete?
- Why were the data originally collected?
- Did the data base serve some hidden political purpose that could induce systematic distortions?
- What procedures are used to deal with missing data?
- Do the computerized records bear a close resemblance to the original records?
- Are some data items periodically updated or purged from the computer file?
- How were the data collected and entered, and by whom?

To have a good idea of quality, the planner should interview the data collectors, observe the data entry process, and compare written records to the computerized version. *Conducting an analysis of administrative records only seems easy if it is not done carefully.*

Observational Data

Observational procedures become necessary when events, actions, or circumstances are the major form of the data. For example, if we are concerned whether the water supply in a given city is safe to drink, we might want to observe the actual testing procedures and determine if all required steps are followed. The data then would take the form of written summaries, typically by the researcher or his or her designee, of the activities that occurred. If the events, actions, or circumstances are repetitive or numerous, this form of data can be very expensive to collect. Because many times the subject of the data collection is complex, detailed guides may be necessary to structure the data collection and summary.

Table 4.1
Procedures Checklist for Evaluating Secondary Data

— Identify potential data source(s)

— Arrange meeting(s) with relevant individuals re data source

— Collect and review information on source re:

its original purpose(s) and use(s)

the types of information available

the specific measures used for pertinent variables (obtain codebook)

methodological aspects of the data collection procedures

specific details of the information sources

the unit(s) of analysis

technical details of the data base (obtain documentation)

— Determine if data source is appropriate with respect to:

the relationship between the concepts and the measures

the population or sample of information sources

the extent of missing data

the unit(s) of analysis

— Revise conceptual model (if necessary)

— Determine if supplemental data are needed

— Finalize analysis approach

— Arrange for transfer of the data

— Conduct preliminary data cleaning analyses

— Verify and/or validate data on all variables to be used

SOURCE: Adapted from Rog and Landis (1985).

Documents

Finally, documentary evidence may serve as the basis for an applied researcher's data collection—documents that allow the researcher to track what happened, when it happened, and who was involved. Examples of documentary data include meeting minutes, journals, program reports, and others. Investigative research may rely on documentary evidence, often in combination with testimonies or interviews.

Documents also may be the raw data base for other, more sophisticated kinds of analysis, such as content analysis. In content analysis, researchers establish content categories and then review documents and code the occurrence of various characteristics (Krippendorf, 1980). The coding procedure is highly structured, tested for intercoder reliability, and applied systematically to written documents. The technique has the ability to transform complex issues into empirical analyses if adequate attention is given to the development of meaningful coding categories. The GAO (1988), for example, used content analysis in a review targeted at determining whether the claims of news censorship were warranted for the Department of Defense overseas newspaper *Stars and Stripes*. The content of *Stars and Stripes* news articles in the European and the Pacific issues were compared with that of the major news wire services during March 1987. The findings that both newspapers ran a lower proportion of stories presenting a negative image of the military than were carried by major wire services led the GAO to recommend actions to strengthen the independence of the *Stars and Stripes* managing editor.

Often it is also through review of documents that researchers establish standards to help address normative questions: determining legislative intent, reviewing regulations and laws, reviewing contract language, or identifying other sources of guidance. In this case, access may sometimes prove to be a problem, especially if a program administrator or staff member is suspected of mismanagement or fraud. At times the researcher is in the dark about the existence of what would be very helpful documents, and therefore he or she cannot even raise the question of access.

Amount of Data

The research planner must anticipate the amount of data that will be needed to conduct the study. The appropriate amount involves decisions regarding data sources, time periods, and number of units (e.g., study participants), as well as the precision desired. As noted in Chapter 3, *statistical conclusion validity* is an important factor in planning research. Such validity is concerned primarily with those factors that might make it appear that there were no statistically significant effects when, in fact, there were effects. The greater the ability of the research to detect effects that are present, the greater the statistical power of the study.

Many planners are not sensitive to the degree to which the study they are planning may be doomed to failure because of insufficient statistical power to detect a meaningful effect. For example, a well-known study of the effects of police patrols found that the presence of police had no effect on victimization rates. It was not noted at that time, however, that the statistical power of the design was so low that if the victimization rate was reduced to zero, it still would not have been statistically significant (Schneider & Darcy, 1984). In this case, the design was not sensitive, and the program may have been branded falsely as a failure when in fact the failure should be laid at the door of the evaluation plan.

Deciding if the results of a study, even if they are statistically significant, are meaningful or trivial is not easy. The size of the effect that is judged to be meaningful will depend on many factors, including the values of the person making the judgment, the cost-effectiveness of the program, and the purpose of the program. As a substitute to trying to obtain this judgment from stakeholders, some general guidelines have been developed to estimate effect sizes.

Technically, *effect size* is defined as the proportion of variance accounted for by the treatment or as the difference between a treatment and control group, measured in standard deviation units. The purpose of using standard deviation units is to produce a measure that is independent of the metric used in the original dependent measure. Thus we can discuss universal effect sizes regardless of whether we are measuring school grades, days absent, or self-esteem scores. This makes possible the comparison of different studies and different measures in the same study. Conversion to standard deviation units is obtained by subtracting the mean of the control group from the mean of the treatment group and then dividing this difference by the pooled or combined standard deviations of the two groups.

To judge whether an effect size is meaningful, some rules of thumb have been developed. The seminal work in this field has been done by Cohen (1977, 1988), who developed the categories for effect sizes for social science research shown in Table 4.2. The table indicates that a small effect size may be considered to be 20% of a standard deviation between the treatment and control group. In variance terms, this indicates that the treatment accounted for 1% of the between-subject differences in the dependent variable (i.e., proportion of variance).

There are a number of factors that could account for not finding an effect when there actually is one. All of these factors affect the statistical power of the design (i.e., the ability to detect an effect when it is indeed present). The most visible factor that affects statistical power is the size of the sample. One of the first questions that researchers usually need to answer is how many subjects are needed for a particular study. If the number of subjects tested is too small, then the researcher risks missing a real effect. If the sample selected is larger than needed to detect a meaningful effect, then resources used for data collection and analysis are wasted. So salient is the concern for sample size that an entire book has been devoted to this issue (Kraemer & Thiemann, 1987).

Table 4.2

Effect Size Categories Designated by Cohen (1977)

Effect Size Category	Effect Size	Proportion of Variance
small	.20	.01
medium	.50	.06
large	.80	.14

Methods for Improving Statistical Validity. Improving statistical validity simply by increasing the sample size is sometimes very costly and sometimes not possible. There are other factors that can and should be considered in designing evaluations so as to improve statistical validity. Lipsey (1990) indicates that there are four factors that govern statistical power: the statistical test, the alpha level, the sample size, and the effect size.

1. *The Statistical Test.* The same data can produce different conclusions, depending upon the particular statistical test used. Parametric tests, like *t* tests, generally have more power than nonparametic tests such as chi-square. Moreover, any statistical procedure that reduces within-group variability (i.e., within the treatment or control group, not between the treatment and control groups) will improve the statistical power of the design (e.g., blocked or covariance designs in analysis of variance).
2. *The Alpha Level.* When conducting a statistical test the researcher usually sets the alpha level (e.g., $p < .05$), or the probability of rejecting the null hypothesis when it is true. The higher or more stringent the alpha level, the less likely it is that the researcher will commit a type I error (i.e., conclude that there was an effect when there actually was not). The probability of making this error is the alpha level. Alpha levels are usually set at probabilities of .05 or .01. The former indicates that if the results were significant, it is likely that only 5 times out of 100 would this be attributable to chance; the latter simply decreases the odds of making this mistake by requiring the results to meet the more stringent criterion of only 1 time out of 100 by chance. The higher the alpha level, however, the smaller the power of the analysis.
3. *Sample Size.* Sampling error is an important factor affecting statistical significance. Smaller samples have greater error associated with them, thus increasing the required size of an effect to achieve statistical significance. As noted in Chapter 3, it is as critical to

remember in study planning that sample size refers to the statistical sampling unit. If a person receives the treatment independently of others, then the individual is the unit of analysis. If the unit that is selected and assigned to the treatment or comparison group is the family, however, then sample size is the number of families and not the total number of persons (i.e., all family members) participating in the study. Misspecification of the unit of analysis often takes place in educational research when classes are assigned to treatment and control groups and the treatment is delivered to the class as a unit, but the investigator uses individual student data in the analysis instead of aggregating the data to the class level.

Increasing sample size seems like an obvious and simple strategy to increase statistical power. Additional subjects are not always available, however, and there is a large cost associated with increasing the size of the sample studied. Not only do additional subjects need to be recruited, but often this requires the addition of new sites or extending the study time so that data from additional subjects can be collected. Additional subjects also will increase the costs of printing questionnaires or paying for more interviewers, paying more subjects, and preparaing and processing more data.

Demonstrating the inadequacies of the sample sizes used in much applied research, Lipsey (1990) found that for the median effect size (.40) in evaluation research, statistical power in a sample of published evaluation studies was .42 (i.e., little more than half the value of .80 recommended by Cohen). This means that the evaluator had less than a 50/50 chance of detecting a real effect. Table 4.3 shows the needed sample size, *per group*, required to detect effects of different sizes given an alpha level of .05. Typically, a power of .80 is an acceptable level of power, although some applied work may require more power to help ensure that a real effect is not labeled incorrectly as statistically insignificant. Thus, if the researcher wishes to detect an effect of size of .60 with a power of .80, then a sample size of about 45 in each group would be needed. If the study is required to detect a much smaller effect (e.g., .30), then a much larger sample size (e.g., more than 175 subjects) would be required. Clearly, selection of sample size is a complex activity, intimately tied to other study design decisions. Table 4.3 can be used as a rough guideline for estimating sample size, but the reader is urged to consult Lipsey (1990) for more information.

4. *Effect Size.* The larger the actual size of the effect, the easier it will be to detect. The size of the effect will depend on two factors. Recall that

Table 4.3

Approximate Sample Size Per Experimental Group Needed to Attain
Various Criterion Levels of Power for a Range of Effect Sizes at Alpha = .05

Effect Size	.80	.90	.95
.10	1,570	2,100	2,600
.20	395	525	650
.30	175	235	290
.40	100	130	165
.50	65	85	105
.60	45	60	75
.70	35	45	55
.80	25	35	45
.90	20	30	35
1.00	20	25	30

SOURCE: Lipsey (1990). Reprinted by permission.

the definition of effect size is the difference between the treatment
and the control group, divided by the standard deviation. Anything
that influences either the size of this difference or the within-group
variance will influence the size of the effect. Effect size can be
enhanced by increasing the difference between the treatment and
control group and/or decreasing the variability within each group.

The difference between the treatment and control groups will be affected
by the integrity of the independent variable. In an evaluation, if the
treatment degrades, then the effect size will be reduced by decreasing the
potential difference between the two groups. Thus the strength and integrity of the treatment (Yeaton & Sechrest, 1987) is important to maintain,
not only for construct validity, but for power reasons as well.

Dependent variables must be valid, sensitive, and accurate to have
good statistical power. Selection of measures is an important aspect of
planning a study. Some measures are more sensitive to detecting effects
than others. For example, if a program attempts to change a child's
self-esteem by 5 points on a particular scale, and the instrument can only
detect changes of 10 points, then it may appear that the program failed even
when it was successful. The measure selected must be not only a valid
measure but also sensitive to change. Floor and ceiling effects—that is,
scores that are either already close to their minimum (floor) or maximum
(ceiling)—can reduce sensitivity to change. In general, norm-based mea-

sures (e.g., standardized achievement tests) are less sensitive to change than criterion-referenced measures (e.g., mastery tests).

In general, continuous measures can detect differences better than categorical measures. The evaluator can increase the reliability of the instrument by aggregating:

- across a large number of data points (or measures) at one time,
- over more points in time, and
- across more individuals.

Composites of measures and scales (see DeVellis, 1991) are more reliable than single indicators or items. As an indication of how reliability can influence effect size, Lipsey (1990) indicates that a reliability of .50 can reduce the effect size to about 70% of the value that would be obtained with a perfectly reliable measure. The researcher may need to conduct pilot studies to examine measurement issues if there is not adequate prior research using the planned instruments on the target population.

Variability in data collection also can affect within-group variance. Because most applied studies are not conducted in laboratories it is difficult, if not impossible, to control or eliminate all extraneous influences. Good training of data collectors, however, can decrease variability. Finally, the heterogeneity of the sample studied increases variability. Some of this variability can be reduced by more narrowly defining the eligibility for participation in the study, being attentive to the potential trade-off of a cost (loss) in generalizability. Statistical techniques, such as blocking (i.e., categorizing the sample into more homogenous groups), can also be used to reduce heterogeneity and thus increase power.

Estimating Effect Size. In general, effect size poses the most difficulty for the research planner. Alpha levels, sample size, and the statistical model can be established easily, but estimating effect size is much more difficult. As noted above, it depends on:

- the strength and fidelity of the treatment,
- the sensitivity of the dependent variables,
- the extraneous variability in the dependent measures, and
- the actual size of the difference between the treatment and control groups.

Lipsey suggests three ways to estimate effect size. First, the investigator can take an actuarial approach to estimating effect size. If there is sufficient research literature, the researcher can use previous studies to compute the effect sizes found in these evaluations. Although effect size is not reported in most studies, the techniques used in meta-analysis can be used to compute effect sizes from a variety of statistics (see Rosenthal, 1991, for procedures). Existing meta-analytic studies can be very useful in predicting effect sizes. There are hundreds of such studies already published. Using these studies, it is possible to have some confidence about what effect size can be expected.

A second approach for estimating effect sizes is to translate or convert existing data statistically into effect sizes. Lipsey (1990) describes how to compute effect sizes from studies that present either normed data, success rates, or proportion of variance explained.

A third method for estimating effect sizes is to set a criterion for success. This would entail establishing the minimum improvement in the dependent variable scores that would constitute a meaningful result. This criterion could be derived through discussions with key stakeholders in the study and/or through discussions with experts and reviews of past research. This approach focuses on the practical significance of the evaluation outcome.

Many research projects fail before the first datum is collected because the design does not have sufficient statistical power to detect the effects of an intervention. Moreover, when researchers have been aware of power concerns, they have believed mistakenly that increasing sample size is the only solution. Increasing the amount of data collected (the sample size) is clearly one route to increasing power; given the costs of additional data collection, however, an increase in sample size should be considered only after the alternatives of increasing the sensitivity of the measures, improving the delivery of treatment, selecting other statistical tests, or raising the alpha level have been explored thoroughly. If planning indicates that power still may not be sufficient, then the researcher faces the choice of not conducting the study, changing the study to address more qualitative questions, or proceeding with the study but informing the clients of the risk of "missing" effects below a certain size.

Whichever route is chosen, power issues need to be discussed thoroughly and openly so that the decision will be an informed one, not one glossed over in the haste to get the research started.

Accuracy and Reliability of Data

Data are useless if they are not accurate and reliable. Whether using extant data or making plans to collect new data, researchers are concerned heavily with the data quality issue. Do the data adequately operationalize the concepts of the study's underlying framework? Can a certain variable be measured accurately, with only small measurement error? If new data collection is planned, how reliable will the results be? If another researcher were to follow these data collection procedures, would he or she obtain similar results?

The concept of *construct validity* (i.e., measuring what one intends to measure) is very relevant here (see Chapter 2). The researcher is concerned that the variables used in the study either are strong operationalizations of key variables in the study's conceptual framework or are reasonable approximations of them. It is a fact of life of applied research that many times researchers have to use "proxy" variables to stand in for the variables they would like to measure. For instance, assume that a researcher is attempting to answer the following question: Are urban public hospitals providing less than optimum emergency room care for critically ill patients because of the increased volume of nonemergency walk-in patients that they are serving? The variable "less than optimum emergency room care" is a very important variable to operationalize for this study.

In this case, it is unlikely that the researcher will develop a comprehensive measurement process for quality of emergency room care; instead he or she will strive to develop proxy measures. Such measures might include (a) adherence to triage guidelines for referring the "sickest" patients to treatment first, (b) average time in waiting room for various emergency patient categories, and (c) ratios of staff/patient density. It makes sense to use proxy measures only if there is empirical evidence linking the variables or if there is a general consensus that these variables are reasonable approximations of optimum care. A research advisory group can be very helpful both in informing the choice of proxy measures and in adding their weight to supporting the research results based on such measures.

The researcher must also be concerned with the possibility of large *measurement errors*. Whenever there is measurement of a phenomenon, there is some level of error. The concept is easiest to illustrate when considering the administration of tests. For example, a health knowledge test for eighth graders is administered and yields a test score (Y) for the individual's knowledge of health education that reflects both his actual knowledge X (true score), if measured perfectly, and some amount of error. The error may be random or systematic. It may reflect the fact that the student stayed out late at the movies the night before and fell asleep during the test or that the test is generally more comfortable for students who frequently take multiple-choice tests. The amount of error may fluctuate across students and across test administrations. It is important to remember that just about all measures contain some degree of error. The challenge of measurement is to minimize it or understand it sufficiently to adjust for this degree of error. If the error is systematic (i.e., not random), the researcher may be able to correct statistically for the bias that is introduced. It is often difficult for the investigator to discover that any systematic error exists, however, let alone its magnitude. Random error can be controlled best by using uniform procedures in data collection. This will require training and monitoring of data collectors.

Design Fit

Even when accurate and reliable data exist or can be collected, the researcher must ask whether the data fit the necessary parameters of the design. Are they available for all necessary subgroups? Are they available for the appropriate time periods? Is it possible to obtain data at the right level of analysis (e.g., individual student vs. school)? Do different data bases feeding into the study contain comparable variables? Are they coded the same way? If extant data bases are used, the researcher may need to ask if the data base is sufficiently complete to support the research. Are all variables of interest recorded in it? If an interrupted time-series design is contemplated, the researcher may need to make sure that it is possible to obtain enough observations prior to the intervention in question, and that there has been consistency in data reporting throughout the analytic time frame.

TYPES OF DATA COLLECTION INSTRUMENTS

Once preliminary ideas can be formulated about the nature of the data, the researcher needs to consider what types of data collection forms will be required. A wide variety of data collection instruments are available to the applied researcher:

- observational recording forms
- tests and standardized scales
- data extraction forms/formats
- structured interview guides
- mail and telephone surveys

Observational Recording Forms

Observational recording forms are guides to requesting and documenting information. The subject may be events, actions, or circumstances that are either live or must be recreated through discussions or review of written documentation. Thus a researcher studying a summer employment program for youths might use an observational guide to record various kinds of activities that occur within the program in a typical week.

Observational recording forms are necessary when there is substantial information to be collected through observational means or when there are multiple data collectors. In the first case, creating a recording guide can help the researcher make sure that all areas have been covered, as well as eliminate the need for recontacting research participants again. This is especially desirable when it is expected that multiple individuals will need to be consulted in order to obtain a complete picture of a phenomenon. Because each person may know only a piece of the picture, and because it may not be clear who these interviewees are in advance, a structured recording form can assist the researcher in obtaining complete information efficiently when making a site visit.

In the second case, the situation of a study employing multiple data collectors, the use of a recording form provides necessary structure to the data collection process, thereby ensuring that all collectors are following similar procedures and employing similar criteria in choosing to include or exclude information. This is especially critical when data collectors are asked to make complex judgments or interpretation of the data on site.

Observational guides frequently are used when researchers study the implementation of a new program or policy, helping them to apply a consistent set of inquiries across multiple sites or time periods. The recording form itself may be in the form of a checklist (e.g., allowing the researcher to check observed features), brief inquiries, or open-ended exploratory questions.

Tests

In applied studies, researchers are more likely to make use of existing instruments than to develop new ones to measure knowledge or performance. The cost of developing a new instrument is generally prohibitive in that the process of test development involves committing substantial resources to create and assess test or scale items, analyze the underlying structure of the test, and norm it on an appropriate population.

Whether choosing to use a test "off-the-shelf" or capitalizing on an existing data base that includes such data, it is very important to be thoroughly familiar with the content of the instrument, its scoring, the literature on its creation and norming, and any ongoing controversies about its accuracy. Especially in the educational and employment areas, extant data bases may include test scores, and strong views often are held by the educational community and special groups about cultural biases for certain tests. In these kinds of situations, decisions have to be weighed carefully as to whether including the test scores offers enough benefit to the research to outweigh a potential controversy.

Data Extraction Forms/Formats

Data extraction forms/formats are a fact of life for applied research. Frequent reliance on administrative records and documents is a major factor underlying the use of this type of data collection. Whether one is obtaining information from manual case records or computerized data tapes, it is necessary to screen the data source for the key variables and record them into the research data base. Sometimes new variables are even created during this process by using other information in a manual or computerized file.

A data extraction form may be a manual coding sheet for recording information out of a paper file folder, or the data collector may use a portable computer to enter information directly into a preformatted research data base. In the former situation, the coding sheets would be scanned or keypunched, and the computerized data would then be available to the researcher. The latter procedure of entering data directly into a computerized form has the advantage that the data are transferred manually only once from their original source.

Even when the original source is computerized, the researcher will still need to engage in creating a data extraction format. He or she will need to identify the relevant variables on the computerized file and then write a program that pulls the appropriate information onto the research file. In circumstances where there are multiple sources of data (e.g., monthly welfare case load data tapes), it may be necessary to apply these procedures to multiple data sources, using another program to merge the information into the appropriate format for analysis.

Structured Interview Guides

Whenever a research project requires obtaining the same information items from multiple individuals, it is desirable to create a structured interview guide. Again, as for observational recording forms, the need for structured data collection processes becomes even greater when multiple data collectors are being used (see Fowler & Mangione, 1989, on standardized survey interviewing).

A structured interview guide may begin with an explanation of the purpose of the interview and then proceed to a set of sequenced inquiries designed to collect information about attitudes, opinions, memories of events, characteristics, and circumstances. The questions may be about the individuals themselves or about activities occurring in their environment (e.g., individual dietary habits, program activities, world events). The guide itself typically is structured to interact with the individual's responses, branching from one area to the next based on the individual's previous answer. Thus a structured interview, depending on how much of the guide is relevant to the individual, may take only 5 minutes to several hours.

Structured in-person interviews are favored in circumstances where it is judged helpful to establish an interview/interviewee rapport in order to obtain the information. This includes situations where the research inquiries are complicated, sensitive, or controversial, and where it is believed the response rates will be low if inquiries are made through telephone or mail surveys. Other qualifying situations include respondents who may not be able to read, unmotivated or actively reluctant respondents, and situations needing translators.

There also are instances in which semistructured or even unstructured interviews may be appropriate. These approaches may be appropriate in descriptive, exploratory research in a new area of inquiry. A topic-centered interview is useful in these situations, posing general topics or questions followed by a number of subtopics or probes that can be used to direct the ensuing discussion.

Mail and Telephone Surveys

Mail and telephone surveys are used when it is necessary to obtain the same information items from large numbers of respondents. They have many parallels to the structured interview data collection, but request information either through a written questionnaire (by mail) or through a telephone interview. Fowler (1988) provides a detailed overview of survey methodology and the various types of surveys, and Fowler and Mangione (1989) focus on how to implement and maintain standardization in survey interviewing. Lavrakas (1987) describes telephone survey methods, including issues of sampling and selecting respondents and supervision of interviewers.

Survey development and design are complex activities, consuming significant resources to develop questions and pretest survey administration. Surveys generally cover a set of structured topics (domains) and contain the same branching features as structured interview guides. Substantial effort may be necessary to determine the most effective wording for questions and to pilot both the specific survey questions and survey administration procedures. This is especially true when conducting international survey work that requires translations or when administering a survey to diverse populations within a single country. Marín and Marín (1991), for example, describe methods for developing, adapting, and translating instruments for Hispanic populations. Therefore a decision to use survey data collection techniques should not be made lightly and should be contemplated only after it has been ascertained that primary data collection is unavoidable. Especially for mail surveys, the effort necessary to develop test items, pilot the survey, revise the survey, administer the survey, and follow up on nonrespondents may consume significant *calendar* time. Unfortunately, many of these tasks must be done sequentially, rather than simultaneously, making it difficult to reduce the length of time needed.

Calendar time for the actual collection of the data can be reduced through the use of telephone surveys, as the researcher does not have to wait for responses to be provided through the mail. Also, if computer-assisted telephone interviewing (CATI) is employed, the survey interviewer can read questions right off a computer screen and record the respondents' answers directly onto a data base. CATI techniques have an advantage over manual coding in that they can significantly reduce interviewer error. This is because the branching that occurs based on respondents' answers can be built directly into the CATI programming. That is, if a respondent answers yes to question 6, the interviewer's screen will automatically branch to question 8 (skipping question 7).

Decisions to rely on survey data collection also need to consider the likelihood of obtaining reasonable response rates. Some populations are very familiar with survey methodology and may be depended upon to complete and/or respond to surveys willingly. Others may be suspicious of anything associated with a "government agency" arriving through the mail, or may require a financial incentive for participation. Some populations are simply not accessible by telephone, either because of residential transience of residence or financial reasons, and therefore cannot be expected to participate in telephone surveys. In these cases, mail surveys are unlikely to be successful either, and the researcher may need to budget to support expensive in-person interviewing or find another method to obtain information on the variables of interest.

DATA ANALYSIS PLANNING

At this point, a tentative design has been chosen, and various approaches to data collection are under serious consideration. Before proceeding on to the time-consuming activities of instrument construction and testing, the researcher should draft a preliminary analysis plan. It is important to do analysis planning prior to data collection for two reasons: (a) to ensure that the design/data collection approach will actually enable the researcher to answer the critical study questions, and (b) to make the study's execution as efficient as possible.

The researcher should chart out carefully the major analyses he or she expects to perform, tying each table, chart, or statistical test back to the major questions, study variables, data collection methods, and data sources. Care should be taken to plan for both the major dependent variables and any controlling variables. For instance, if the research uses a quasi-experimental nonequivalent groups design, it may be necessary to include in the statistical analysis variables that can be used to make corrections for any incomplete "equivalencies" in the groups. Thus in evaluating a program intended to raise the likelihood of employment of teenage youths, it would be useful to have information available concerning presence or absence of any previous work history for all members of the treatment (program participants) and comparison groups. Even with randomized designs, where groups are assumed to be equivalent through random assignment, the analyst should engage in worst-case scenario planning to ensure that if the randomization procedures fall apart, sufficient information will be available to enable other analysis approaches to be tried. Planning for potential adjustments needs to occur up front; waiting until the analysis is under way will be much too late.

Text continued on page 92

Table 4.4

Data Collection Framework (partial)

	Data Sources			Data Collection Methods		
	Documents	Parents	Children	Document Review	Telephone Interview	Focus Groups

Research Question

What is the nature of the target population?

Variables

Description of screening and selection process:
— nature of screening process
— demographic data on families screened but not selected
— eligible criteria
— exclusion criteria
— definition of homelessness
— definition of families
— strategies for engaging families

Data Sources			Data Collection Methods		
Documents	Parents	Children	Document Review	Telephone Interview	Focus Groups

Description of families:

— family size
— family composition (including children in foster care)
— housing history (3 years):
   —housing status
   —participation in HUD programs
   —past evictions
   —reasons for evictions
— family relationships and social supports
— family disruptions
— entitlement history
— current entitlements
— service use (prior to project)
— service needs
— barriers to service use

Table 4.5
Design Matrix

Issues/Request Specifications	Questions	Information Required	Source of Information
This column will vary in content. Issues may be global or highly specific. There may be references to "impact," "costs," or "effectiveness." USE DIRECT QUOTES FROM THE REQUEST LETTER OR STATUTE WHERE APPLICABLE.	Key Words: Who? What? Why? How? When? Where? How much? To what extent? Notes: — Make sure each question asks only one question. — Sequence questions in logical order. — Nest the questions where applicable. — Use direct quotes from request letter or statute where applicable.	Preliminary Matrix: Broad identification of information required, i.e., pre/post cost data; extent of client satisfaction with program; policies and procedures, etc. Detailed Matrix: Specific identification of information required, i.e., which policies and procedures, names of other (external) studies, internal audits, item identified cost data (dates), etc.	Preliminary Matrix: Agency officials (name agency) Files (name agency, site) Data tape (agency/ database name) Client categories Contractor categories Other subject categories/groups Document review Detailed Matrix: Names/site of specific agency officials Detailed information on which files Specific name of tape, file identifiers, timeframes Names of clients Names of contractors Names of other subjects Specific citations of documents

Table 4.5

Continued

Data Collection Methods	Analysis	Comments

USE ACTION VERBS
 	
Tasks are actions you can visualize people doing.
 	
Key words:
 	
Interview
Review
Develop/administer/ analyze DCI (including mail questionnaire & structured interview)
Obtain
Describe
Calculate
Verify
Contact
Analyze data
Determine relationships
Survey
	This column pinpoints general type of analysis as well as the specific analytic techniques used.
	
	Key words:
	
	Preliminary matrix—
	  Description
	  Tabulation
	    Frequencies
	    Percentages
	  Determine decision rules
	  Compare, compare/contrast
	  Cost analyses
	    Cost/benefit
	    Cost-effectiveness
	    Cost/utility
	  Identify
	  List
	  Trend analysis
	  Map
	  Modeling
	
	Detailed matrix—
	  Cross-tabs
	  Time series
	  Survival analysis
	  Regression analysis
	  Other multivariate techniques
	  Modeling (specify)
		Anything pertinent can be said here. Of particular interest will be comments about:
		
		— Data availability and quality
		— Time (to collect data, do analyses, build models, etc.)
		— Generalizability/ limitations on what can be said with the information we gather
		— Known reality being contrary to assumptions made in the request
		— Quality/quantity of staff needed
		
		This column can also be used to highlight areas "yet to be determined." For example, when you know you must evaluate a particular policy, but the standards are presently unknown, make comments about "Criteria?" in the Comments column.

Early analysis planning permits more efficient and economical study execution by tightly targeting data collection. Data collection is one of the most expensive activities of applied research, and major unnecessary costs can accrue from collecting data that are not needed. Drafting an analysis plan can enable the researcher to determine exactly how the information will be used, allowing for elimination of unneeded survey questions, file searches, and the like, along with their attendant travel and mailing costs. Unfortunately, some researchers only feel comfortable when they have surrounded themselves with stacks of information about a given issue, problem, or program, striving to create the illusion that they have comprehensive and conclusive information. Although it is always desirable to think through fallback data collection and analysis strategies and to build in triangulation on key constructs (i.e., multiple measures of a single construct), unfocused data collection is unjustifiably expensive. It consumes resources often better spent elsewhere, makes it harder to focus the analysis, undoubtedly makes study execution longer, and creates only a short-lived illusion of competence.

Table 4.4 presents an example of a data collection framework. The data collection framework is designed to display each research question and the specific variables that relate to each question, and the data sources and data collection methods that will be used to collect the information. The table illustrates this process for one question: What is the nature of the target population? The actual matrix includes other variables (description of parents and children), as well as other questions. This type of framework, when developed in the research design phase, offers a detailed blueprint for developing each data collection instrument. In developing the framework, the researcher can more readily determine where triangulation will occur and where an excessive burden on any one data source may need to be reduced.

Table 4.5 displays a companion "design matrix" that displays, in abbreviated form, the overall study issues, research questions, information needed, data sources, data collection methods, analyses planned, and any special comments. This matrix was developed to guide study design planning at the GAO (Johnson, 1988) and is recommended for use early on in the design process to ensure that all pieces of the planned data collection and analysis activities tie back to the study questions. It is a good tool for identifying gaps in the logic of a study plan.

5

Resource Planning

Most books on research methods do not discuss the resources needed to conduct the research, nor is this topic usually covered in courses on research. Applied research, however, requires the consideration of the realistic constraints on the research process. This chapter is intended to assist the researcher in dealing with the constraints imposed by the limited resources common in almost all research. Before making final decisions about the specific design to use and the type of data collection procedures to employ, the investigator must take into account the resources available and the limitations of these resources. In addition, all resource planning must be performed in the context of real-life external deadlines. For example, sound information produced after a legislative deadline for action loses much of its value. Planning and care in implementing the research can be as important as the research questions asked. It is an integral part of the iterative Stage II planning activities (see Figure 5.1).

This chapter will describe how to consider resource questions before making final design and data collection decisions. In particular, this chapter will consider the following resources:

- *Data:* What are the sources of information needed and how will they be obtained?
- *Time:* How much time is required to conduct the entire research project and its elements?
- *Personnel:* How many researchers are needed and what are their skills?
- *Money:* How much money is needed to plan and implement the research and in what categories?

It should be noted that this chapter, because of space limitations, cannot deal with the critical issue of where and how to obtain resources to conduct applied research. The reader is directed to other sources, such as the chapter by Baron (1987) in *The Compleat Academic,* or the *APA Guide to Research Support* (Herring, 1987).

AUTHORS' NOTE: This chapter is adapted from Bickman, L. (in press). "Resource planning for field research," in F. Bryant, J. Edwards, L. Heath, E. Posavac, & R. S. Tindale (eds.), *Methodological Issues in Applied Social Psychology.* New York: Plenum.

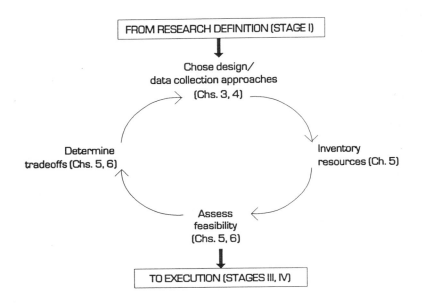

Figure 5.1. Stage II: Development of a Research/Design Plan

DATA AS A RESOURCE

The most important resource for any research project is the data used to answer the research question. Data for research can be obtained primarily in two ways: from original data collected by the investigator, and from already existing data. The issues of primary data collection will be discussed first, followed by secondary data analysis.

Primary Data Collection

This section addresses major issues in planning for primary data collection: site selection, authorization, the data collection process, accessibility, and other support needed.

Site Selection. Applied and basic research differ on a number of dimensions, as discussed in Chapter 1, but probably the most salient difference is the location of the research (Bickman, 1981). In most cases, basic research will take place in a site that is controlled by the investigator, often a psychological laboratory or a college classroom. Applied research can occur in diverse settings. Sometimes the site is specified by the research question, as when the researcher is asked to assess the functioning of a specific program. In other cases, the investigator has the option of choosing among one or more sites.

The selection of appropriate sites is of utmost importance to the success of the project. For example, Grady and Wallston (1988) devote a chapter in their book on health research to a description of heath care settings. They point out that health care settings differ in terms of whether they are concerned with sickness or wellness and, if the former, whether they focus on acute care, chronic care, or rehabilitation. The choice of setting will determine the types of individuals or patients studied and the events to observe. The setting will have a clear impact on the research not only in defining the population studied, but also in formulating the research question addressed, the research design implemented, the measures used, and the inferences that can be drawn from the study. For example, if we were studying the correlation of age with certain sicknesses, we would come to different conclusions if we studied the elderly in Golden Age Clubs rather than in nursing homes. The latter will have sicker and less independent individuals. Choosing settings can also determine whether there are enough research participants available. Thus a researcher would usually not want to select a health club to evaluate a new smoking cessation program, because most of the members of the club probably do not smoke.

Deciding on the appropriate number and selection of sites is an integral part of the design/data collection decision, and a decision that often has no single correct answer. Is it best to choose "typical" sites, a "range" of sites, "representative" sites, the "best" site, or the "worst" site? There are always more salient variables for site selection than resources for study execution, and no matter what criteria are used, research critics will claim that other important variables (or other *more* important variables) were omitted. For this reason, it is recommended that the site selection decision be done in close coordination with the research client and/or advisory group. In general, it is also better to concentrate on as few sites as are required, rather than stretching the time and management efforts of the research team across too many locations.

Another example of an emphasis on settings is provided by the text by Jorgensen (1989) on participant observation. Jorgensen characterizes settings as differing in visibility and openness. A visible setting is one that is available to the public. Some of these settings, such as universities and hospitals, may be visible enough to be listed in the phone directory. Other visible settings may be less public but still accessible, such as areas that involve drugs or prostitution that police know about. Invisible settings are hidden and concealed from outsiders. These settings include both legal and illegal activities. In most organizations, there are groups of individuals whose activities are kept secret from nonmembers and, in some cases, even from members. A setting's openness will depend upon the degree of negotiation that is required for access, but visibility and openness are not the same. A university is a visible institution, but the deliberations in the provost's office concerning faculty salaries are not open to the faculty, let alone the general public. Highly visible settings may also contain less visible activities; for example, public parks are often a location for illicit sexual activities.

A distinction of "frontstage" and "backstage" made by Goffman (1959) also helps distinguish settings. Frontstage activities are available to anyone, whereas backstage entrance is limited. Thus the courtroom in a trial is the frontstage activity that is open to anyone who can obtain a seat. Entrance to the judge's chamber is more limited, presence during lawyer-client conferences is even more restricted, and presence as an observer during jury deliberations is impossible. The researcher needs to assess the openness of the setting before taking the next step: seeking authorization for the research.

Authorization. Even totally open and visible settings usually require some degree of authorization for data collection. Public space may not be as totally available to the researcher as it may seem. For example, it is a good idea to notify the authorities if the research team is going to be present in some public setting for an extended period of time. Though the researcher's presence is certainly not illegal and does not require permission to conduct observations or interviews, residents of the area may become suspicious and call the police. For example, in one of our studies, interviews were conducted in a rural area. The interviewers, being unfamiliar with the area (which lacked street signs), drove through the same stretch of road repeatedly looking for particular houses. Residents, not accustomed to seeing strange cars, called the sheriff. The interviewers were stopped and taken to the sheriff's station for questioning. Calls were made to the university to verify the interviewers' legitimacy. A simple letter or call to each local law enforcement office could have prevented this problem.

If the setting is a closed one, the researcher will be required to obtain the permission of the individuals who control or believe they control access. If there are a number of sites that are eligible for participation, and they are within one organization, then it behooves the researcher to explore the independence of these sites from the parent organization. In planning a study of bystander reactions to staged shoplifting (Bickman, 1984; Bickman & Rosenbaum, 1977), cooperation of the supermarket in which the crime was to be staged had to be obtained. There was the choice of contacting the headquarters of the company or approaching each supermarket manager for permission to conduct the study. If the main office was approached first and we were refused permission, then the project could not be implemented. If one local manager refused, however, then another one could be approached. In this case, we first approached a local manager, who informed us that he could not participate without headquarter's approval. The manager, however, was persuaded to provide a supporting letter to accompany our request for permission. A personal visit to the head of security helped obtain the necessary cooperation.

Not only does the planner need to know at which level of the organization to negotiate, but also which individuals to approach. Again, this will take some intelligence gathering. Personal contacts help, because authorities are usually more likely to meet and to be cooperative if the researcher is recommended by someone they know and trust. Thus the investigator should search for some connection to the organization. If the planner is at a university, then it is possible that someone on the board of trustees is an officer of the organization. If so, contact with the university's development office is advisable. Is the organization part of the federal bureaucracy? If so, then a phone call to your congressional office might help. The idea is to obtain advance recommendations from credible sources and hence to avoid approaching an organization cold.

Permission from a central authority does not necessarily imply cooperation from the sites needed for data collection. Nowhere is this more evident than in state/county working relationships. Often central approval will be required to approach local sites. The investigator should not believe, however, that central approval guarantees cooperation from those lower down on the organization's hierarchy, as this can lead the investigator into behaving in an insensitive manner. Those at the upper levels of an organization tend to believe they have more power than they actually wield. A wise investigator will put a great deal of effort into obtaining cooperation at the local level. At this level are the individuals who feel they control that environment and with whom the investigator will be interacting during the data collection phase. The persons in this environment will include not only management but the workers and their representatives (e.g., unions). Keeping them informed of the purpose and progress of the study and what is happening to and in *their* environment should be a high priority.

Some closed organizations have procedures that must be followed if they are going to issue permission to conduct research in their setting · (e.g., prisons and schools). Confidentiality and informed consent are usually significant issues with any organization. Will participants be identified or identifiable? How will the data be protected from unauthorized access? Will competitors learn something about the organization from this research that will put it at a disadvantage? Will individuals in the organization be put in any jeopardy by the project? These issues need to be resolved before approaching an organization for permission.

Confidentiality issues can be very complex in applied research. In conducting an evaluation of the AFDC program, for example, the GAO found that it was a violation of Massachusetts state law if field interviewers, in seeking to locate former AFDC recipients, let it be known to any other persons that the individual they were seeking was or ever had been a recipient of public welfare monies. The state sent periodic reminders that the project director could be fined if there was any evidence that such disclosures had been made. Needless to say, training of interviewers heavily emphasized the confidentiality issue, and interviewers were not allowed to discuss with anyone other than the respondent the purpose of their survey.

Organizations that have experience with research usually have standard procedures that they follow with researchers. For example, school systems typically have standard forms to complete and deadlines by which these forms must be submitted. These organizations understand the importance of research and are accustomed to dealing with investigators. In contrast, other organizations may not be familiar with applied research; most for-profit corporations fall in this category. In dealing with these groups, the investigator will first have to convince the authorities that research, in general, is a good idea and that their organization will gain something from their participation. Most important, the organization has to be convinced that it will not be taking a significant risk in participating in the study. The planner must be prepared to present a strong case as to why a nonresearch-oriented organization should want to involve itself in a research project.

Finally, any agreement between the researcher and the organization should be in writing. This may be an informal letter addressed to the organization's project liaison officer (there should be one) for the research. The letter should describe the procedures that will take place and indicate the dates that the investigator will be on-site. The agreement should be detailed and include how the organization will cooperate with the research. This written agreement may avoid misunderstandings that are based on past in-person or telephone discussions (i.e., "I thought you meant . . .").

Data Collection Process. Gaining access for primary data collection is just the start of the planning process. Careful attention then needs to be paid to the details of the study. These include recruiting the participants and the logistics required at the site.

1. *Participants.* The primary purpose of obtaining access to a site is to be able to collect data from or about people. The researcher should *not* assume that having access ensures that the target subjects will agree to participate in the study. Moreover, skepticism is warranted in accepting the assurances from management concerning others' willingness to participate in a study. For example, in an evaluation of a nutrition program for the elderly (Bickman, 1985), cooperation was obtained from the federal agency that funded the program and from each local project manger to implement and evaluate a program. Each local manager furnished the number of elderly persons in their site and estimated the percentage that they thought would participate in the study. Random assignment of sites to treatment and control conditions proceeded based on these estimates. During the recruitment phase of the data collection, it was clear that the study would fall far short of the required number of subjects. The design of the study was jeopardized when new sites had to be recruited to increase the sample size.

In a review of 30 randomized studies in drug abuse, Dennis (1990) found that 54% seriously underestimated the client flow, by an average of 37%. Realistic and accurate participant estimates are necessary to allocate resources and to ensure sufficient statistical power. This latter point often has been ignored in the past, however. Research by Lipsey, Crosse, Dunkle, Pollard, and Stobart (1985) found that 90% of the 122 evaluation studies reviewed had insufficient statistical power to detect small effect sizes, and 60% did not reliably find a medium effect if it was present. Rossi (1990) expressed similar concerns about the low power of psychological research in his review of 221 articles published in three psychological journals. He concluded that low power contributes to the difficulties many investigators experience in replicating other's work. Many funding agencies are now insisting that power analyses be conducted when submitting grant proposals. Moreover, these power analyses should be supported by evidence that the number of cases used in these analyses are valid estimates.

Planners can try to avoid shortfalls in the number of cases or subjects needed by conducting a small pilot study (Boruch & Wothke, 1985). In a pilot study, the researcher can verify enrollment and attendance data, as well as willingness to participate. Thus an investigator who wishes to collect data from students in a college classroom is well advised to learn not only the number of students enrolled in the course but how many, on the average, show up for class. In some cases this may be less than half of those enrolled. To estimate the percentage that would be willing to participate, it is advisable to ask potential subjects if they would take part in a study similar to the one planned. Alternatively, the investigator may be able to gauge the participation rate from the experiences of other researchers.

In cases where potential subjects enter into some program or institution, it will be important to verify the actual subject flow (e.g., number per week). For example, if the study requires participation of subjects who are receiving psychotherapy, then it is critical to know how many *new* patients enter the program each week. This will establish the maximum number of subjects that could participate in the study. By estimating the volunteer rate of new patients entering therapy, the planner can judge the total amount of time needed to conduct the study. If that total time proves too long, the planner will know that additional sites need to be recruited. Related to the number of participants is the assurance that the research design can be implemented successfully. Randomized designs are especially vulnerable to implementation problems. It is easy to promise that there will be no new taxes, that the check is in the mail, and that a randomized experiment will be conducted. It is often difficult to deliver on these promises. In an applied setting, the investigator should obtain agreement from authorities *in writing* that they will cooperate in the conduct of the study. This agreement must be detailed, be procedurally oriented, and clearly specify the responsibilities of the researcher and those who control the setting.

2. *Logistics.* The ability to implement the research depends on the ability of the investigator to carry out the planned data collection procedures. A written plan for data collection is critical to success, but it does not guarantee effective implementation. A pilot or "walk-through" of the procedure is necessary to determine if it is feasible. In this procedure, the investigator needs to consider the following:

a. *Accessibility.* There are a large number of seemingly unimportant details that can damage a research project if they are ignored. Will the research participants have the means to travel to the site? Is there sufficient public transportation? If not, will the investigator arrange for transportation? If the study is going to use an organization's space for data collection, will the investigator need a key? Is there anyone else who may use the space? Who controls scheduling and room assignment? Have they been notified? When using someone else's space, it is important to make certain that the investigator is able to control it during the time it is promised. For example, a researcher about to collect posttest data in a classroom should ensure that he or she will not be asked to vacate the space before data collection is completed.

b. *Other Support.* Are the light and sound sufficient for the study? If the study requires the use of electrical equipment, will there be sufficient electrical outlets? Will the equipment reach the outlets, or should extension cords be brought? Do the participants need food or drink? How will these be provided? Are there rest-room facilities available? Are the surroundings quiet enough to conduct the study? Can necessary modifications be made in the environment to conduct the study? Is the environment safe? Are there enough chairs, pencils, space, forms, and assistants available to collect the data? If the data collectors are in the field, do they have proper identification? Are the appropriate persons in the home organization aware of the study and the identity of the data collectors? Are those persons prepared to vouch for the legitimacy of the research? Is there sufficient space not only to collect the data but to house the research team, assemble the data collection instruments, and analyze and store the data? Space is a precious commodity in many institutions; do not assume that the research project will have sufficient space. Obtain a commitment from those who control space in the planning phase and *before* a grant proposal is submitted.

Secondary Data Analysis

Another approach to conducting applied research is to use already existing data, as noted in Chapter 4. This has the advantage of lower costs and time savings but may also entail managing a large amount of flawed and/or inappropriate data. In some cases, these data will exist in a format that is designed for research purposes. There are a number of secondary data sources developed by university consortia, federal sources such as the Bureau of the Census, and commercial data such as *Inform,* a data base of 550 business journals. In other studies, the data will exist as administrative records that were *not* designed to answer research questions. This section deals primarily with using a record system for secondary data analysis; more information about secondary research can be obtained from Stewart (1984).

In the planning process, the investigator must have confidence that the records contain the information that is required for the study. Assurances from authorities are helpful, but a direct examination of a representative sample of records should be conducted. Sampling records will provide the researcher with an indication not only of the content of the records, but also of their quality. It is frequently the case that clinical or administrative records are *not* suitable for research purposes. First, the records may be stored in a way that makes them inaccessible for research purposes. For example, there may not be a central collection point for all records, thus increasing the costs of collecting data. Second, if the records are computerized, this may be of tremendous advantage to the investigator, but not all the information that was collected on paper may be transferred to the computer data base. The investigator needs to confirm the availability and content of records needed for the research.

The planner must also have some confidence in the quality of the records. Are the records complete? Why were the data collected originally? The data base may serve some hidden political purpose that could induce systematic distortions. What procedures are used to deal with missing data? Do the computerized records bear a close resemblance to the original records? Are some data items updated or purged periodically from the computer file? How were the data collected and entered, and by whom? To have a good idea of quality, the planner should interview the data collectors, observe the data entry process, and compare written records to the computerized version. Conducting an analysis of administrative records, as was noted earlier, only seems easy if it is not done carefully.

To gain access to a record system, the investigator also must demonstrate how the confidentiality of the records will be protected. If the records contain client names, then there is a significant risk associated with providing those records to a researcher. If individual names are not necessary, the organization may be willing (often at a cost) to provide sanitized records with personally identifying information removed. In cases where the names are not important to the researcher but it is important to link individuals to the data base or to data collected later, then a computerized linking file should be established that the providing organization can use to link names with researcher-established identification numbers.

Finally, the investigation should not assume that the level of effort needed to process extant data will be small or even moderate. Data sets may be exceedingly complex, with changes occurring in data fields and documentation over time. Specific expertise may be necessary in certain programming languages, and the time necessary to check, clean, and merge data and create working analysis files can be enormous.

TIME AS A RESOURCE

Time takes on two important dimensions in planning applied research—*calendar* and *clock* time. Calendar time is the total amount of time that is available for the project. Calendar time varies across projects: It may be a semester for a course-related research project, 3 years for an externally funded research grant, or 2 weeks for a research contract. The calendar time can substantially influence the scope of a research project.

Time and the Research Question

The calendar time allowed in a study should be related to the research questions (see Kelly & McGrath, 1988, for an extended discussion of how time relates to the research question). Is the phenomenon under study something that lasts a long period of time, or does it only exist for a brief period? Does the phenomenon under study occur in cycles? Is the time allocated to data collection sufficient?

The first consideration of time, therefore, is to examine its relationship to the phenomenon that is being studied. For example, if the event to be studied occurs infrequently and for a short period of time, and if it is somewhat unpredictable, then a long period of calendar time may be needed to capture enough occurrences of this event. If the study deals with physical aggression on the streets, for example, and if the investigator wants to study this phenomenon by observing it, then under most circumstances a long period of observation would be needed. In fact, the nature of this infrequent and unpredictable event would probably rule against using observation as a data collection technique. Other times, dependent phenomena may take a long period of time to unfold and manifest themselves. Thus a drug treatment program that takes a lengthy period for the effects of the treatment to materialize would require a long period of study if the investigator wanted to document an impact. If the phenomenon is cyclical in nature, then the researcher should plan the length of the data collection period to include the various cycles to obtain an accurate representation of the phenomenon. If the project is an evaluation of a program, then the evaluator may need to wait for the program to stabilize before collecting data. Until this initial stage is completed, the program may be highly variable in its operation. Calendar time needs to be allocated in the research for this aspect of program development. All these points argue that in planning an applied research project, the investigator must have some familiarity with the phenomenon under study. The researcher may fail to implement a good study if the relationship between time and the subject studied is not considered.

Time and Data Collection

The second way in which time should be considered is in terms of the actual or real *clock time* needed to accomplish some task. The event that is being studied might exist infrequently and only for a short period of time; thus we might need a long period of calendar time devoted to the project, but only a short period of clock time for data collection. As will be noted in subsequent parts of this chapter, estimating time is related to many other estimates made during the planning of research. Once having established the time estimates, the investigator needs to estimate how long it will take for actual data collection. In computing this estimate, the researcher should consider questions of recruitment, access, and cooperation. For example, if a study is being conducted in a hospital setting using patients, the planner should determine the criteria for inclusion in the study, calculate how many patients would meet those criteria, and estimate the percentage of the patients that would volunteer to participate in the study. An estimate of attrition or dropout rates from the study is also needed. If high attrition is predicted, then more time is needed for data collection to have sufficient statistical power. Thus, in computing time, the investigator should have an accurate and comprehensive picture of the environment in which the study will be conducted.

Time Budget

In planning to use any resource, the researcher should create a budget that describes how the resource will be allocated. Both calendar and clock time need to be budgeted. To budget calendar time, the duration of the entire project must be known. In applied research, the duration typically is set at the start of the project and the investigator then tailors the research to fit the length of time available. There may be little flexibility in total calendar time on some projects. A report may be needed for a legislative decision, or the contract may specify a product at a certain time.

Funded research projects usually operate on a calendar basis; that is, the project will be funded for a specific amount of time. This sets the upper limit of the time budget. The investigator then plans what he or she believes can be accomplished within that period of time. Students will usually operate with semester or quarter deadlines. Again, the project will need to be tailored to the amount of time available; the exceptions for students are theses and dissertations that typically have no fixed deadlines. Regardless, the work often expands to fit the time available. Researchers must be able to specify the project scope and approach to fit a limited time frame. A mistake many researchers make in estimating the time budget is to underestimate the time needed, which often results in the late delivery of their products.

The second time budget refers to clock time. How much actual time will it take to develop a questionnaire or to interview all the participants? It is important to decide what unit of time will be used in the budget. In other words, what is the smallest unit of analysis of the research process that will be useful in calculating how much time it will take to complete the research project? To answer this question, we now turn to the concept of tasks.

Tasks and Time

To "task out" a research project, the planner is required to list all the significant activities (tasks) that must be performed to complete the project. The tasks in a project budget are similar to the expense categories needed in planning a personal financial budget. The financial budget is calculated on various categories such as rent, utilities, food, and so on; when listing all of these expense items, an implicit decision is made concerning the level of refinement that will be used. For example, under the food budget, it is rare for a family to categorize their food budget into vegetables, meat, fruit, and milk products. On the other hand, a family might decide to divide the food budget into eating in restaurants versus the purchasing of food for home consumption. In a similar vein, the investigator needs to decide what categories will be used to plan the research.

Table 5.1
Major Tasks of a Typical Research Project

Task 1	Conduct literature review and develop conceptual framework
Task 2	Develop design and instruments
Task 3	Construct sample frame and select sample
Task 4	Collect data
Task 5	Analyze data
Task 6	Write report

Table 5.1 shows an example of an abbreviated task outline for a research project. It shows the major tasks proceeded by an action verb. These major tasks usually are divided into finer subtasks; the degree of refinement depends on how carefully the investigator needs to budget. When the estimates need to be very precise, tasks should be divided more finely. For experienced investigators, the very refined process might not be necessary. A more refined task outline, however, can serve as a useful tool in determining the staffing needs of a project and in guiding the actual implementation of the project.

Conceptual Development. To construct a time budget, the investigator needs to list all the tasks that must be accomplished during the research project. Typically these can be grouped into a number of major categories, as shown in Table 5.1. The first category usually encompasses conceptual development. This includes literature reviews and thinking and talking about the problem to be investigated. Time needs to be allocated for consulting with experts in areas where investigators need additional advice. The literature reviews could be categorized into a number of steps ranging from computerized searches to writing a summary of the findings. Investigators might also want to include in this category the conduct of meta-analytic reviews that involve the quantitative integration of empirical studies. Books by Rosenthal (1984) and Cooper (1989) provide details about this process.

Instrument Development. The second phase found in most projects is instrument development and refinement. Regardless of whether the investigator plans to do intensive face-to-face interviewing, self-administered questionnaires, or observation, time needs to be allocated to search for, adapt, or develop relevant instruments used to collect data. Time also needs to be allocated for pilot testing the instruments. In pilot testing, preliminary drafts of instruments are used in the field with persons similar to the participants in the study. Some purposes of pilot testing are to ascertain the length of time needed to administer the instrument, to check on ease of administration, to practice coding of information, and to determine if there are ambiguities in the ways respondents interpret the instrument.

Pilot testing should never be left out of any project. Typically, there will be "new" flaws that were not noted by members of the research team in previous applications of the instrument. Respondents often interpret instruments differently than researchers. Moreover, widespread use of an instrument does not ensure that participants in your research project will interpret the instrument in the same way. In addition, pilot tests should involve testing out the procedures (training procedures, contact procedures, etc.) as well as testing the instruments.

If the data collection approach involves extracting information from administrative records, pilot testing must take a different form. The researcher should pilot test the training planned for data extractors and test the data coding process. Checks should be included for accuracy and consistency across coders.

When external validity or generalization is a major concern, the researcher will need to plan especially carefully the construction of the sample. The sampling procedure describes the potential subjects and how they will be selected to participate in the study. This procedure may be very complex, depending upon the type of sampling plan adopted. Henry (1990) provides the new investigator with an excellent description of sampling methods.

Data Collection. The next phase of research is usually the data collection. Data collection can include many techniques. For example, the study may involve reviewing previous records (see Stewart, 1984). The investigator needs to determine how long it will take to gain access to those records, as well as how long it will take to extract the data from the records. It is important to ascertain not only how long it will take to collect the data from the records, but whether information the investigator assumes is on those records is there. Records kept for administrative purposes often do not match research needs. Careful sampling and inspection of those records in planning the project are necessary steps to avoid the embarrassment of inability to complete the project because of a lack of data. In planning research, assumptions about data need to be recognized, questioned, and then checked carefully.

If the researcher is planning to conduct a survey, the procedure for estimating the length of time needed for this process could be extensive. Fowler (1988) describes the steps needed in conducting a survey. These include developing the instrument, recruiting and training interviewers, sampling, and the actual collection of the data. Telephone interviews require some special techniques that are described in detail by Lavrakas (1987). This chapter cannot go into depth about these and other data collection methods, other than to indicate that time estimates need to be attached to each task associated with data collection.

Data Analysis. The next phase usually associated with any research project is data analysis. Whether the investigator is using qualitative or quantitative methods, time must be allocated for the analysis of data. Analysis not only includes statistical testing using a computer, but also the preparation of the data for computer analysis. Steps included in this process are cleaning of the data (i.e., making certain that the responses are readable and are not ambiguous for data entry personnel), physically entering the data, and checking for the internal consistency of the data. For example, if a subject said no in response to a question about whether he eats meals out of the home, there should be no answers recorded for that subject about the types of restaurants that he frequents. Other procedures typically included in quantitative analysis are the production of descriptive statistics (i.e., frequencies, means, standard deviations, and measures of skewness). More complex studies may require conducting inferential statistical tests. Analytic procedures for qualitative data collection procedures need to be tailored for the specific project. The reader is referred to books by Jorgensen (1989), Denzin (1989), Fetterman (1989), and Schwandt and Halpern (1988) for further guidance.

Reporting Results. Finally, time needs to be allocated for communicating the results. Applied research projects typically require a final report; this report is usually a lengthy, detailed analysis. Because most people do not read the entire report, it is critical to include a two- or three-page executive summary that succinctly and clearly summarizes the main findings. In applied research projects, the lay audience typically is not concerned with statistical tests, methodology, or literature reviews. These individuals just want to know what was found. The quality of the findings cannot be interpreted, however, without an understanding of the methodology and analysis. The executive summary should focus on the findings and present these as the highlights of the study. No matter how much effort and innovation went into data collection, the procedures are of interest primarily to other researchers and not to typical sponsors of applied research. The best the researcher can hope to accomplish with the latter audience is to educate them about the limitations of the findings based on specific methods used.

The investigator should allocate time not just for producing a report, but also for verbally communicating this information to sponsors. Verbal communications may include briefings as well as testimony to legislative bodies. Moreover, if the investigator desires to have the results of the study utilized, it is likely that time needs to be allocated to work with the sponsor and other organizations in interpreting and applying the findings of the study. This last utilization-oriented perspective often is not included in planning a time budget.

Time Estimates

Once the researcher has described all the tasks and subtasks, the next part of the planning process is to estimate how long it will take to complete each task. This is a difficult process unless there are previous data upon which to base these estimates. One way to approach this problem is to reduce each task to its smallest unit. For example, in the data collection phase, an estimate of the total amount of interviewing time is needed. The simplest way to estimate this total is to calculate how long each interview should take. Pilot data are critical to developing accurate estimates. If pilot interviews took an average of 2 hours each to complete, and if the study calls for 100 interviews, then simple arithmetic indicates that 200 hours need to be allocated for this task. Does this estimate, however, include everything that is important? Is travel time included? Are callbacks to respondents who are not home part of this estimate? Is the time required for editing the data and coding open-ended responses included? Another example is data entry time. It is relatively easy to compute how many keystrokes a data entry person can complete in an hour and then simply divide this by the number of keystrokes needed for the entire project. This computation is a rough estimate, because data from complex instruments will take longer to enter than data from less complex instruments. Pilot testing for data entry is very useful if this task is going to be a major time (and therefore financial) expense of the project.

Whatever estimate the investigator derives, it is likely to be just that: an estimate. There will be a margin of error associated with this estimate. Whether the estimate is too conservative or liberal will depend in part on the context in which the planning needs to occur. For example, if the researcher is planning to compete for a research contract, then it may be the case that an underestimate will occur, as competition may place pressure on the planner to underestimate the costs of conducting the research. On the other hand, inexperienced individuals operating under no particular time pressure (e.g., graduate students) may overestimate time required for conducting a research project. As a rule of thumb, underestimates are more likely and more costly than overestimates. If the research sponsor can afford the time and the money, it would be safe to add an extra 10% to 15% to any estimate. Clearly, this addition indicates a lack of certainty and precision. Do not despair, though; even with many years of experience, highly paid planners in defense firms overrun their contracts frequently.

The clock time budget simply indicates how long it will take to complete each task. What this budget does not tell you is the sequencing and the real calendar time needed for conducting the research. Calendar time can be calculated from the above estimates, but the investigator will need to make certain other assumptions. For example, if the study uses interviewers to collect data and 200 hours of interviewing time are required, the length of calendar time needed for this will depend on a number of factors. Most clearly, the number of interviewers will be a critical factor. One interviewer will take a minimum of 200 hours to complete the task, whereas two hundred interviewers can do it in 1 hour. The larger number of interviewers, however, may create the need for other mechanisms to be put into place (e.g., interviewer supervision and monitoring), as well as create concerns regarding the quality of the data. Thus one needs to specify the staffing levels and research team skills for the project. This is the next kind of budget that needs to be developed.

PERSONNEL AS A RESOURCE

Skills Budget

Once the investigator has described the tasks that need to be accomplished, the second step is to decide what kinds of people are needed to conduct those tasks. What characteristics are needed for a trained observer or an interviewer? What are the requirements for a supervisor? What skills does a data analyst need? Who will be able to manage the project and write the reports? These questions need to be considered in planning a research project. To assist the investigator in answering these questions, a skills matrix should be completed. The matrix shown in

Table 5.2 describes the requisite skills needed for the tasks and attaches names or positions of the research team to each cluster of skills. Typically, a single individual does not possess all the requisite skills, and so a team will need to be developed for the research project. In that case, the labels are simply "economist," "statistician," and so on.

In addition to specific research tasks, management of the project needs to be considered. This function should be allocated to every research project. Someone will have to manage the various parts of the project to make sure that they are working together and that the schedule is being met. To return to the example about the number of interviewers, it is not reasonable, unless the individual subjects are dispersed geographically, to use 200 interviewers for 1 hour each simply because of the excessive amount of time that would be needed to supervise and train that many interviewers. The first consideration is how many individuals can be recruited, supervised, and trained to carry out certain tasks. Second, how finely can tasks be categorized so that more individuals can accomplish them? For example, it is sensible to use multiple interviewers but not to use multiple data analysts. One person might be best working full-time to conduct the data analysis. On the other hand, one person working full-time doing all the interviews would not be recommended. Considerations of time available, skills, supervision, training, continuity of project staff, and burnout are all relevant in computing the next table: the number of hours per person to be allocated for each task.

Person Loading

Once the tasks are specified and the amount of time required to complete each task is estimated, it is necessary to assign these tasks to individuals. The assignment plan is described by a person-loading table (Table 5.3). This table shows a more refined categorization of the tasks needed to develop instruments. The left-hand side of the table lists the tasks required for the project. The top of the table lists all the individuals, or categories of individuals, who will be needed to accomplish these tasks. The example shows that the specification of data needs will be conducted by the project director for 10 hours and require 20 hours of secretarial support. Locating existing instruments will be done by the research assistants working a total of 40 hours each. The interviews will be conducted by the research assistants, with 10 hours of supervision by the project director, for a total of 40 hours each. The statistician will be involved in two tasks: specifying data needs (10 hours) and analyzing interviews (15 hours). This table allows the investigator to know if

Table 5.2
Skills Matrix

Skills

Person	Research Design	Case Methods	Sampling	Institutional Development	Cost Analysis	Statistics	Interviewing
Director	X	X		X	X		X
Statistician	X		X		X	X	
Economist				X	X	X	
Research Assistant		X					X
Research Assistant	X		X	X	X	X	X

Table 5.3
Person Loading Chart

Personnel

	Director	Research Assistant	Economist	Statistician	Secretary	Research Assistant
Task 2.	**Develop Instruments**					
2.1	Specify Data Needs	10	—	5	10	20	—
2.2	Review Existing Instruments						
2.21	Locate Instruments	—	40	—	—	—	40
2.22	Evaluate Instruments	20	20	—	—	10	20
2.3	Construct Instrument-Need Matrix	20	20	—	—	5	20
2.4	Develop New Instruments						
2.41	Develop Interviews	20	20	—	—	30	30
2.42	Conduct Interviews	10	40	—	—	—	40
2.43	Analyze Interviews	10	40	—	15	—	40
2.44	Construct Scales	20	50	—	—	30	50
2.45	Field Test Instruments	10	40	—	—	—	40
TOTAL (hours)		120	270	5	25	95	280

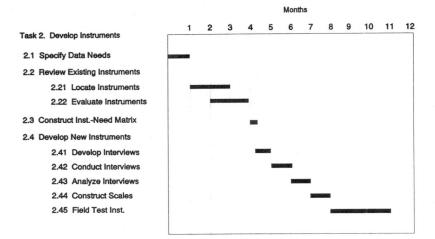

Figure 5.2. Gantt Chart

(a) the right mix of skills will be present in the research team to accomplish the tasks, and (b) if the amount of time allocated to each individual to conduct those tasks is reasonable. Both of these, the skills and the time, will be necessary in developing the next planning tool.

Gantt Charts

We need to return to real, or calendar, time at some point in the planning process, given that the project will be conducted under real time constraints. Thus the tasking chart needs to be superimposed on a calendar. The allocation of calendar time to each task and subtask is shown in Figure 5.2. The figure is called a Gantt chart. It simply shows the tasks on the left-hand side and months on the top of the chart. Each bar shows the length of calendar time allocated for the completion of specific subtasks. This does not mean that if a bar takes up 1 month, the task will actually take a whole month of clock time to complete. The task might only take 15 hours but need to be spread over a full month.

The Gantt chart shows not only how long each task takes, but also the approximate relationship in calendar time between tasks. Although inexact, the chart can show the precedence of research tasks. A more detailed and exact procedure is to produce a PERT chart showing the dependency relationships between tasks. These charts typically are not needed for the types of research projects used in social sciences.

One of the key relationships and assumptions made in producing a plan is that individuals will not work more than 40 hours a week. Thus the person-loading chart needs to be checked against the Gantt chart to make sure that the task can be completed by those individuals assigned to it within the period specified in the Gantt chart. This task is more complex than it seems, because individuals typically will be assigned to multiple tasks within a specified time. It is important to calculate, for each individual involved in the project, how much actual calendar time he or she will be working for all the tasks to which he or she is assigned. Individuals should not be allocated to more tasks or time than can be handled. Very reasonably priced programs that can run on microcomputers are available to help the planner do these calculations and draw the appropriate charts. At this point in the planning process, the investigator should have a very clear estimate of the time budget. The time budget and person-loading chart both are needed to produce a financial budget, which is the next step in the planning process.

FINANCIAL RESOURCES

Usually the biggest part of any research budget is personnel—research staff. Social science research, especially applied social science, is very labor-intensive. Moreover, the labor of some individuals can be very costly. To produce a budget based on predicted costs, the investigator needs to follow a few simple steps.

Based on the person-loading chart, the investigator can simply compute total personnel costs for the project by multiplying the hours allocated to each individual by their hourly cost. The investigator should compute personnel costs by each task. In addition, if the project crosses different years, then the planner will need to provide for salary increases in the estimate. Hourly cost typically includes salary and fringe benefits; if the investigator needs to break out costs by month, this procedure will allow that as well. Table 5.4 illustrates personnel costs for each task. The figures used in this table are for illustrative purposes only and are not meant to represent current salaries for these individuals. Budgets for contracts usually follow this procedure. For grant applications from academic institutions, these calculations will not be necessary; however, they are recommended to be able to plan and monitor a project adequately.

Table 5.4
Personnel Costs

	Director	Research Assistant	Economist	Statistician	Secretary	Research Assistant
Total (hours)	120	270	5	25	95	280
Hourly rates	$40	$10	$40	$40	$8	$11
Total costs	$4,800	$2,700	$200	$1,000	$760	$3,080

Total personnel costs $12,540

Table 5.5 illustrates how other items need to be allocated to the budget to include such cost items as computer time, supplies, duplication, postage, telephone, and travel. In computing how much needs to be allocated in each one of these areas, the same type of analysis used for personnel should be applied. For example, for the duplication costs, the investigator should consider how many pages will be duplicated and the cost of each page. Thus, if the study includes a 10-page questionnaire to be distributed to 200 individuals, then 2,000 pages at 5 cents each should be allocated for this task, for a total of $100.00. The investigator might want to include some additional funds for extra copies and for errors in duplication. The same type of calculation can be used to produce cost estimates for reports. Five reports may be needed, with an estimate of 100 pages each and 20 copies of each report. This costs a total of $500 for duplication. If the report includes covers and binding, these expenses would need to be added to the cost.

Travel costs can be estimated in a similar fashion. If travel is going to be by air to a specific location, then a travel agent can provide the cost of each trip. Given the complex fare structures available, the investigator might want to use an average cost or, to be on the safe side, the maximum regular air fare. If the research team is going to visit a number of places across the country that cannot be specified until the project is funded, then a scenario needs to be developed. Such a scenario could include computing average fares to 10 or 12 likely places to visit. In computing the budget then, one simply takes the average cost of travel to these 10 places and multiplies it by the number of visits and number of persons making visits. The use of a personal car typically is reimbursed at a fixed rate per mile. To estimate meals and lodging, calculate the average cost of meals and hotel stays in that particular city at a cost per day. Some contracts may specify a per diem or the maximum amount that can be spent on food and lodging per day.

The investigator needs to examine the tasks to determine if there are any special costs associated with the project, For example, if a telephone survey is going to be conducted, then it is critical to compute this part of the budget accurately. If a mailed questionnaire is the method, then postage for initial mailings, return mail, follow-up reminders, and other correspondence must be computed. Similarly, if there is going to be a great deal of mainframe computer time expended, then the investigator needs to estimate accurately the amount of time needed to conduct the analysis. Help usually can be obtained from the computer center at a university in calculating these figures.

Table 5.5
Other Direct Costs

	Travel	Telephone	Postage	Duplication	Supplies	Computer	Other
Task 2. Develop Instrument							
2.1 Specify Data Needs							
2.2 Review Existing Instruments							
2.21 Locate Instruments		100	25	10			
2.22 Evaluate Instruments							
2.3 Construct Instrument-Need Matrix							
2.4 Develop New Instruments							
2.41 Develop Interviews							
2.42 Conduct Interviews	200 miles × .26 = $52	25		1,000 copies × .05 = $50	50		
2.43 Analyze Interviews						150	
2.44 Construct Scales							
2.45 Field Test Instruments	200 miles × .26 = $52	10		2,000 copies × .05 = $100		200	
	$104	$135	$25	$160	$50	$350	
Total other direct costs							$824
Total personnel costs							$12,540
Total direct costs							$13,364
Overhead (50% of direct costs)							$6,682
Total costs							$20,046

118

After computing personnel and other costs, institutions usually have an indirect or overhead cost added to the direct expenses of the project. This is the cost associated with conducting research that cannot be allocated to each specific project. These typically include costs for space, utilities, and maintenance, as well as those associated with the university's or firm's management and accounting systems related to grants and contracts. Indirect costs will vary from institution to institution and should be included as part of the budget. For-profit firms also will add a profit percentage to a contract.

In calculating a budget, the distinction between academic and nonacademic settings should be kept in mind. Researchers in academic institutions are not accustomed to calculating personnel budgets as described. Instead, an estimate is made about how many people would be needed or what percentage of time a faculty member is willing to devote to a project, and that is included as part of the budget. This often is a workable solution because the faculty time is fairly flexible. Thus, when the workload of one project is underestimated, the faculty member may just work harder or longer on that project and not spend as much time on other activities. To have an accurate estimate of personnel time required for a project, however, the procedure described above is recommended.

After the budget has been calculated, the investigator may be faced with a total cost that is not reasonable for the project, either because the sponsor does not have those funds available or because the bidding for the project is very competitive. If this occurs, the investigator has a number of alternatives available. The most reasonable alternative is to eliminate some tasks or to reduce their scope. For example, instead of interviewing 200 persons, interview 100. Alternatively, keep the number of persons interviewed the same, but cut back on the length of each interview to reduce costs. There is, of course, a limit how far the project can be cut back. For example, a series of tasks that grossly underestimate the amount of time required will not be evaluated favorably by knowledgeable reviewers. The underestimate will simply indicate to the reviewers that the investigator does not have the capability of conducting the research because he or she was not very realistic about the amount of time or resources required. Another alternative to reducing the size of the budget is to use less expensive staff. The trade-off is that a more expensive staff usually is more experienced and should be able to accomplish a task in less time. Using less experienced staff, however, should result in an increase in the amount of time allocated to conduct that task. The investigator might also want to look for more efficient methods of conducting the research. For example, the use of matrix sampling (where individuals receive different parts of questionnaires) may reduce costs. If a randomized design is possible, it may be feasible, but often very risky, to collect only posttest data and eliminate all pretest data collection. The investigator needs to use ingenuity to try to devise not only a valid, reliable, and sensitive project, but one that is efficient as well.

The financial budget, as well as the time budget, should force the investigator to realize the trade-offs that are involved in applied research. Should the investigator use a longer instrument at a higher cost, or collect less data from more subjects? Should the subscales on an instrument be longer and thus more reliable, or should more domains be covered with each domain composed of fewer items and thus less reliable? Should an emphasis be placed on representative sampling as opposed to a purposive sampling procedure? Should the researcher use multiple data collection techniques, such as observation and interviewing, or should the research plan include only one technique, with more data collected by that procedure? These and other questions are ones that any research planner faces. When under strict time and cost limitations, however, the saliency of these alternatives is very high.

MONITORING PROJECT IMPLEMENTATION

Finally, the investigator should be sure to include in the planning phase methods by which the project can be kept on schedule. Budgetary responsibility requires at least monthly accounting of the expenses. The detailed Gantt chart can be very helpful in determining whether the project is slipping behind schedule. It is often the case that what is implemented in the field does not follow what was planned. The purpose of the planning is not to force a rigid structure on the field operations, but to anticipate and minimize difficulties. Unless some standard is developed and applied, the investigator cannot be sure that the project is tracking correctly. The use of these planning tools as management tools can help the researcher obtain the goal of a competently conducted project.

6

Making Trade-Offs and Testing Feasibility

At this point, the researcher has formulated a preliminary design and research plan that promise to answer a focused set of study questions. Before making a firm go/no-go decision, it is worth taking the time to assess the strengths and weaknesses of the proposed approach and decide whether it is logistically feasible. As noted throughout this text, the process of developing a design is seldom straightforward and linear (see Figure 6.1).

This chapter returns to a discussion of the iterative process that researchers typically use as they assess and refine the initial design approach. Two major activities take place: identifying and deciding on design trade-offs, and testing the feasibility of the proposed design. As portrayed in Figure 6.1, these activities almost always occur simultaneously. Their results may require the researcher to reconsider the potential design approach or even to return to the client to renegotiate the study questions.

MAKING DESIGN TRADE-OFFS

Design planning for basic and applied research inevitably involves making trade-offs. Even in laboratory settings, there are trade-offs that must be made in terms of resources, design, and measurement. In applied research settings, there are many more factors that can force trade-offs; examples of areas where they often occur are external generalizability of study results, conclusiveness of findings, precision of estimates, and comprehensiveness of measurement. Trade-offs often are forced by external limitations in dollar and staff resources, staff skills, time, and the quality of available data. They are part of the reality of applied research and should not necessarily be viewed as negative. Not all study questions warrant either large expenditures of resources or the most comprehensive and sophisticated designs. To a great degree, the worth and credibility of the final study is a function of the researcher's

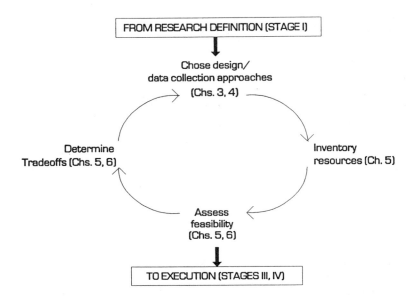

Figure 6.1. Stage II: Development of a Research/Design Plan

skill in balancing trade-offs. Doing this well requires carefully thinking through the implications of each trade-off before making final decisions.

In this section, several types of trade-offs are described and discussed briefly. Examples of the balancing logic are provided, illustrating both positive and negative outcomes. The three themes of credibility, usefulness, and feasibility—the criteria on which trade-offs should be based—appear throughout this discussion.

External Generalizability

External generalizability refers to the extent to which research findings can be proposed credibly as applicable to a wider setting from the research setting. For example, if one wants to describe the methods used in vocational computer training programs, one might decide to study a local high school, an entire community (including both high schools and vocational education agencies and institutions), or the nation. These choices vary widely with respect to the resources required and the effort that must be devoted to constructing sampling frames. The latter two choices (i.e., an entire community or the nation) would

require creating a list of the universe of relevant institutions and programs from which to sample and might, in fact, require conducting a
preliminary survey to identify relevant schools, agencies, and universities. The trade-offs here are ones of both resources and time. Local
information can be provided much more inexpensively and quickly;
however, it will not be known whether the results obtained are representative of the methods used in other high schools or used nationally.

Sometimes other types of compromises are made. Perhaps the client
would like to know about programs operating beyond the local community but does not care if the information is representative nationally. In
this case, communities might be chosen in states with quite different
training approaches, simply with an idea of exploring the degree of
diversity in teaching methods. In such a case, the results from each
community would be summarized separately, each one treated as a
separate case. This type of approach could be quite useful to a local or
state agency wishing to educate itself as to the kinds of programs it
might consider. It is very important in such a situation that great care is
taken in choosing the communities and that the client and the researcher
have a clear understanding of the limits of the generalizability of such
an approach in advance of the fieldwork.

The choice of study scope is tied closely to the phrasing of the study
questions—whether the client is concerned only with local programs
and whether he or she is interested in only high school-based programs
or also desires information on adult education programs. When the
client has no clear preference, this is an area where the researcher has
the flexibility to narrow the study scope to a more manageable, but still
meaningful, level of generalizability.

Generalizability can refer to time dimensions as well as geographic
and population dimensions. For example, many government-funded
programs report data on a regular basis to states or to the federal
government; even so, such data may become outdated rapidly. The
Nationwide Food Consumption Survey is conducted only periodically;
thus a researcher asked to provide current information on households'
food purchasing habits may find that the most recent data are 5 years
old. Making decisions regarding whether to rely on these data versus
collecting new data requires investigating whether there are any reasons
to expect that food consumption patterns would have changed in the last
5 years, as well as discussions with the client as to the reasons for
wanting current data.

Generalizability decisions need to have considerable stakeholder
involvement. Stakeholders need to have a *clear* understanding of the

generalizability boundaries at the initiation of the study. One strategy for communicating these boundaries is to provide stakeholders with scenarios of the research results, illustrating what types of conclusions can and cannot be made on the basis of the current design.

Conclusiveness of Findings

One of the key questions is how confident we need to be in the correctness of the findings, that is, how conclusive the study must be. Research often is categorized as to whether it is exploratory or confirmatory in nature. An exploratory study might seek only to identify the dimensions of a problem, such as the types of drug abuse commonly found in a high school population. In this case, a study might take the form of an initial survey to identify types of drug abuse, which might then be assessed more systematically and on a broader scale in subsequent research. More is demanded for a confirmatory study. In this case, the researcher and client have a hypothesis to test, such as that among high school students use of marijuana is twice as likely as abuse of cocaine or heroin. In this example, it would be necessary to measure with confidence the rates of drug abuse for a variety of drugs and test the observed differences in rate of use.

The decision as to whether an exploratory or confirmatory study is needed should be one of the issues discussed with the client when the original study questions are refined. Moving to an exploratory study, however, is also an option during the design phase. If the resources necessary to conduct a confirmatory study are not readily available, or if the information needed to design a solid confirmatory study is nonexistent, the researcher may wish to raise this issue again during design planning. Sometimes we do not know enough about a problem to support the design of a confirmatory study. For example, we may not know enough about the types of drug abuse found in certain cities to create survey instruments, or we may not have sufficient information to posit hypotheses about the relative prevalence of various types of drug abuse. In the latter case, it may not be possible to estimate required sample sizes sufficient to administer surveys. Again, this is an instance where the researcher may advocate a trade-off. The client's information needs might be better met through an exploratory study, with the decision to mount a larger-scale effort deferred until the exploratory study's results have been obtained.

Precision of Findings

In choosing design approaches, it is essential to have an idea of how small a difference or effect it is important to be able to detect for an evaluation, or how precise a sample to draw for a survey. This decision drives the choice of sample sizes and sensitivity of instrumentation and thus affects the resources that must be allocated to the study. For example, in comparing samples of high school vocational education programs and vocational education programs for adults, do we want to be able to detect 20% differences in the use of on-the-job training methods or differences as small as 5% in the use of such methods? The sizes of the groups required to detect differences in training methods used will be a function both of the actual distribution of the character-istic and of the size of the difference one wants to detect. It will be necessary to study more programs to detect smaller differences.

In the case of vocational education programs, the client may be quite satisfied if the design approach enables detecting only large differences, but for other research topics it may be desirable to detect quite small differences. For example, if one were studying the effect of a low-cost drug abuse prevention program, it could be argued that even achieving a 5% reduction in heroin addiction would be more than sufficient to justify the expense of the program, both in reducing future dollar costs to society and in improving the quality of peoples' lives. Thus a larger investment of resources could be supported to detect this smaller effect.

Sampling error in survey research poses a similar issue. The more precise the estimate required, the greater the amount of resources needed to conduct a survey. If a political candidate feels that he or she will win by a landslide, then fewer resources are required to conduct a political poll than if the race is going to be close and the candidate requires more precision or certainty concerning the outcome as pre-dicted by a survey.

Comprehensiveness of Measurement

The last area of choice involves the comprehensiveness of measure-ment used in the study. This is a different issue from the question of study scope discussed in Chapter 2. It deals not with whether all relevant questions are answered, but with the degree to which multiple measures are used to study the same phenomenon.

It is usually desirable to use multiple methods or multiple measures in a study, for this allows the researcher to look for consistency in results, thereby increasing confidence in findings. Multiple measures, however, can sometimes be very expensive and potentially prohibitive. Thus researchers frequently make a trade-off between resources and comprehensiveness in designing measurement approaches.

A good example of this type of situation can be found in the employment and training research literature. If one desires to assess the effects of a training program on subsequent employment, there are several kinds of strategies that may be used: access to data on individuals' use of unemployment insurance; individual quarterly-earnings records on the state employer wage-contribution files; surveys, telephone, or in-person interviews with individuals; and interviews combined with review of pay receipts. Obviously, these strategies involve different levels of resources; they also can result in different measures and different levels of information. Unemployment insurance records will provide the grossest information (whether or not persons have sought unemployment benefits subsequent to having been in a training program). State wage data will provide more detailed information about more people. These data permit obtaining information about the amounts of earnings obtained during a fixed period; however, even they will not disclose whether there has been an episode of unemployment during that period. Interview strategies allow the gathering of much more detailed information, such as employment status on a weekly basis as well as earnings. Finally, interviews in combination with review of pay receipts allow for obtaining detailed *verified* information on employment and earnings for continuous periods of time.

Choosing the most appropriate strategy involves making trade-offs between the level of detail that can be obtained and the resources available. Calendar time to execute the study also may be relevant. Surprisingly, the use of administrative data can sometimes even take longer than collecting new survey data, because the use of secondary sources of data will sometimes involve substantial time lags before all data have been entered into administrative data systems. These types of trade-offs need to be assessed thoroughly and discussed with the client before the final design decisions are made. Within the measurement area, the researcher often will have to make a decision about breadth of measurement versus depth of measurement. Here the choice is whether to cover a larger number of constructs, each with a brief instrument, or study fewer constructs with longer and usually more sensitive instrumentation. For example, the researcher may be interested in the effects of a school health education program on children. The program may affect knowledge, attitudes, and behavior. If the researcher tries to tap into all three areas with a brief questionnaire, then there is a risk that each construct will not be measured reliably, and no effects may be detected. The simplest way to improve the reliability of measurement is to increase the number of items that measure that construct. The researcher needs to decide if all three areas are equally important or to try to maximize the chances of finding effects in one or two constructs by eliminating the other constructs from the survey.

Thus the trade-off between comprehensiveness (breadth) or depth is almost always made in research. The researcher should be sensitive to this trade-off. Trade-offs occur not only between approaches and resources but among elements of design. Thus, within fixed resources, a decision to increase external validity by broadening the sample frame may require a reduction in resources in other aspects of the design. The researcher needs to consider which aspects of the research process require the most resources.

FEASIBILITY TESTING
OF THE RESEARCH DESIGN/PLAN

Once a design tentatively has been selected, the researcher must determine whether the design is feasible. Throughout the previous chapters, areas to be tested for feasibility have been highlighted. They include the assessment of any secondary data, pilot tests of data collection procedures and instruments, and pilot tests of the design itself (e.g., construction of sampling frames, data collection procedures, and other study procedures). In addition, efforts may be needed to explore the likelihood of potential confounding factors (i.e., whether external events are likely to distort study results or whether the study procedures themselves may create unintended effects). The process of feasibility testing may take as little as a few hours or may involve a trial run of all study procedures in a real-world setting and last several weeks or months.

Through feasibility testing, the researcher learns whether the research approach is likely to maintain its integrity or whether it is likely to fall apart. Additional research issues also may become evident during this process, sometimes requiring consultation with the research clients or audiences. The end result is a go/no-go decision to use the preliminary design, sometimes necessitating a return to the drawing board if the decision is no.

The premise of feasibility testing is that, although sometimes time-consuming, it can greatly improve the likelihood of success or, alternatively, can prevent resources from being wasted doing research that has no chance of answering the posed questions. A "no-go" decision does not represent a failure on the part of the researcher but instead an opportunity to improve on the design or research procedures, and ultimately it results in better research and (it is hoped) better research utilization. A "go" decision reinforces the confidence of the researcher and others in the utility of expending resources to conduct the study.

Because many of these topics have been discussed in detail in previous chapters, we mention only a few of them here as reminders.

Assessment of Secondary Data

Any researcher planning to use secondary data, whether developed by other researchers or drawn from administrative data files, needs to know the accuracy and reliability of the data. Is it an appropriate data source? Answering this question is part of the feasibility test, for if the data source fails, it can no longer be considered the basis for the study. The second part of the feasibility test concerns whether the data are usable. Can the researchers obtain access to the data in a manner that includes all necessary variables? Is the documentation sufficiently clear to interpret all variables? If the coding of the data changed over time, is it possible to obtain information on the changes and standardize values of variables across time? Answers to these questions determine whether use of secondary data is feasible.

Pilot Tests of Data Collection Instruments

Whenever data collection instruments are used in a study, they should be pilot tested during the planning phase. Pilot testing ensures that the instruments are designed optimally to capture all required research information. It is our experience that no matter how well researchers believe they know an area when they first design a data collection instrument, pilot testing will yield several needed changes. Sometimes it is changing the wording of a question to make sure that survey respondents have the same understanding of the item as the researchers. Other times, it simply is clarifying the coding instructions so that the data collectors all follow consistent procedures. Periodically, the pilot test will indicate such significant problems that the entire instrument will need to be restructured or the choice of data collection approach revisited. This is not an area to consider cutting back when trying to economize or save time, for any time saved at the beginning is likely to be more than lost at the end.

Pilot Tests of the Design

Besides pilot testing the data collection instruments, researchers need to pilot test the design itself. Generally, this involves testing the feasibility of proposed sampling plans, testing data collection procedures, and/or testing randomization or treatment procedures.

First, if the research design/plan involves sampling, questions need to be asked concerning whether the needed sampling frame exists. For example, if the plan is to create a comparison group of all AFDC mothers in the state of Massachusetts who worked during September 1991, and the researcher plans to use administrative records from September 1991 as the sampling frame, it needs to be determined if the archived monthly AFDC data tapes contain any useful variables denoting earned income. If yes, it may be possible to use this tape as the sampling frame; if no, the researcher may have to look for another data source or potentially revise the design if there is no such source.

Second, assuming that it is possible to design a sound data collection instrument, the next step is to try out the planned data collection procedures. How will respondents be contacted? What level of cooperation can be expected? If low cooperation is anticipated, the researcher may need to consider including strategies to increase cooperation. Options discussed previously include working with community groups to achieve their endorsement of the research, or even using incentives (cash, food, or gifts) to make participation more attractive.

Third, attention needs to be paid to the execution procedures of the study. If randomization is planned, trial runs may be mounted to make sure that those tasked with carrying out the random assignment procedures do so correctly and do not deviate and allow "special exceptions." Trial runs may also be necessary to make sure that the treatment can be implemented as intended. If the study is of a new intervention, the researcher will need to make sure that all services are ready and will be available to the first study enrollee. If the study is of a new diet regimen, there may be no point mounting randomization into new-diet versus regular-diet groups until it can be determined if people can stick to the new diet long enough to allow a test of its merits. Otherwise, if the treatment group significantly deviated from the diet, the study would not be an accurate reflection of the diet's merits. The treatment itself would have been implemented incompletely.

Identification of Potential Confounds

Prior to moving to execution, the researcher should make one final effort to identify any potential confounds to the research design/plan and estimate (qualitatively or quantitatively) their likely influence on results. Confounds may be external (e.g., a dramatic increase in a community's unemployment rate because of the closing of the community's major employer) or internal, generated by the design itself. Randomization procedures may sometimes create low morale in control groups and guilt in those groups receiving a potential valuable treatment or service. Pretesting may sensitize respondents to a particular topic, thus heightening the influence of the treatment that follows.

A CHECKLIST FOR APPLIED RESEARCH PLANNING

Once the researcher has balanced any design trade-offs appropriately and determined the feasibility of the research plan, final discussions are held with the client to confirm the proposed approach. If agreement is obtained, the research planning phase is complete. If agreement is not forthcoming, the process may start again with a change in research scope (questions) or methods.

Throughout this text, we emphasized the iterative nature of applied research planning and illustrated it repeatedly with a circular model of planning showing how the process may loop back on itself periodically as new information is uncovered or further discussions with the client clarify the focus of the research. Table 6.1 provides a somewhat different summary of the planning process in the form of a checklist. Although a checklist cannot illustrate the interdependence of the planning activities, it does enable us to provide an abbreviated summary of the many tasks that we believe must be carried out during the planning process. Most of the included tasks refer to major activities discussed in the previous chapters. Others we include as reminders, for they refer to tasks that, unfortunately, are overlooked frequently.

We wish you well as an applied researcher and hope that you will have found this text to be both informative and useful. Doing applied

Table 6.1

Checklist for Applied Research

Stage I: Defining the Focus of the Research

Understand the issue
  — Hold discussions with research client; discuss initial costs.
  — Review the literature.
  — Gather current information from experts and other interested parties.
  — Conduct site visits.

Identify the research questions
  — Categorize research questions.
      (descriptive, normative, correlative, impact)
  — Clarify client interest in recommendations.
  — Identify and define key terms/study variables.

Refine/revise the research questions
  — Develop a conceptual framework.
  — Categorize questions as primary or subordinate.
  — Negotiate study scope with client/consumer.
  — Determine any scope limitations.

Establish credibility with client/consumer
  — Maintain continuous communication.
  — When appropriate, negotiate interim products.
  — Form advisory group.
  — State study limitations up front.

Stage II: Developing a Research Design/Plan

Select a preliminary research design
  — Create descriptions of key variables and how they are expected to be related.
  — Define study population.
  — Determine the appropriate level of measurement.
  — Define desired degree of generalizability (population, geography, time).
  — Determine needed level of precision.
  — Consider descriptive, experimental, and quasi-experimental design options.
  — Outline the analytic comparisons required to answer the research questions.
  — Select preliminary approach.

Select preliminary data collection approaches
  — Identify likely sources of data.
  — Confirm amount of data that are available.
  — Determine the form of the data.
  — Assess the likely accuracy and reliability of extant data or new data to be collected.
  — Consider how well/poorly the data fit the preliminary design.
  — Consider need for development of data collection instruments:
      observational recording forms,
      tests,
      data extraction forms/formats,

(continued)

    structured interview guides, and
    mail and telephone survey instruments.
— Develop, pilot, and finalize data collection instruments.
— Draft preliminary analysis plan.
Conduct resource planning
  If primary data collection, consider the following:
    — Select data collection sites.
    — Obtain authorization for data collection from all levels at all sites.
    — Develop sound estimates for numbers of study participants.
    — Develop time estimates for recruiting and training data collectors.
  If secondary analysis, consider the following:
    — Obtain access to the data.
    — Explore the fit and feasibility of the data.
    — Check data for relevance, accuracy, reliability, and completeness.

Develop task plans for *clock* and *calendar* time
    — Identify time boundaries stemming from the research questions.
    — Prepare a task outline of the research activities.
    — Develop a Gantt chart for all major tasks, showing calendar time estimates.
    — Check time estimation to make sure time has been allowed for:
        data cleaning,
        analysis,
        reporting,
        follow-up, and
        project management.

Develop plan for personnel resources
    — Prepare skills matrix.
    — Allocate personnel time across project tasks.
    — Prepare a person-loading chart.

Develop plan for financial resources
    — Use person-loading chart to compute personnel costs.
    — Allocate costs by task for other resources:
        computer time,
        supplies,
        duplication,
        postage,
        telephone, and
        travel.
    — Develop budget monitoring procedures.

Determine final design/plan
    — Assess strengths and weaknesses (credibility and usefulness) of the preliminary design/plan.
    — Assess feasibility of preliminary design, data collection approach, and resource plan.
    — Refine/revise as necessary design/plan.
    — Discuss final design/plan with client, noting any limitations.
    — Make go/no-go decision on whether to move to Stage III: implementation.

research in the complex real world truly is much more difficult than working in a research laboratory. Nevertheless, the rewards of teasing out a credible and useful answer to a significant societal question greatly outweigh the difficulties. The key to conducting sound applied research is planning, and the key to planning can be found in all the tasks we have described in previous chapters. We hope that the lessons we have learned over the years as applied researchers will help you to minimize or avoid any pitfalls.

References

Baron, R. A. (1987). Research grants: A practical guide. In M. P. Zanna & J. M. Darley (Eds.), *The compleat academic*. New York: Random House.

Bickman, L. (1981). Some distinctions between basic and applied approaches. In L. Bickman (Ed.), *Applied social psychology annual* (Vol. 2). Newbury Park, CA: Sage.

Bickman, L. (1984). Bystander intervention in crimes: Theory, research and applications. In J. Karylowski, J. Rekowsky, E. Staub, & D. Bar-Tal (Eds.), *Development and maintenance of prosocial behavior: International perspectives*. New York: Plenum.

Bickman, L. (1985). Randomized experiments in education: Implementations lessons. In R. Boruch (Ed.), *Randomized field experiments, No. 28. New directions for program evaluation* (pp. 39-53). San Francisco: Jossey-Bass.

Bickman, L. (1987). The functions of program theory. In L. Bickman (Ed.), *Using program theory in evaluation* (pp. 5-18). San Francisco: Jossey-Bass.

Bickman, L. (1989). Barriers to the use of program theory: The theory-driven perspective. *Evaluation and Program Planning, 12*(4), 387-390.

Bickman, L. (Ed.). (1990). *Advances in program theory*. San Francisco: Jossey-Bass.

Bickman, L., & Henchy, T. (1971). *Beyond the laboratory: Field research in social psychology*. New York: McGraw-Hill.

Bickman, L., & Rog, D. (1986). Stakeholder assessment in early intervention projects. In L. Bickman & D. Weatherford (Eds.), *Evaluating early childhood intervention programs*. Austin, TX: Pro-Ed.

Bickman, L., & Rosenbaum, D. (1977). Crime reporting as a function of bystander encouragement, surveillance, and credibility. *Journal of Personality and Social Psychology, 35,* 577-586.

Blinder, A. S. (1991, May 27). Economic viewpoint: If you think teen motherhood causes poverty . . . think again. *Business Week*, p. 20.

Boruch, R. F., & Cordray, D. (1985). Professional codes and data sharing. In Committee on National Statistics, National Research Council, *Sharing research data*. Washington, DC: National Academy Press.

Boruch, R. F., & Wothke, W. (Eds.). (1985). *Randomization and field experimentation*. San Francisco: Jossey-Bass.

Brekke, J. S. (1987). The model-guided method for monitoring program implementation. *Evaluation Review, 11,* 281-299.

Campbell, D. T., & Stanley, J. (1966). *Experimental and quasi-experimental designs for research*. Chicago: Rand McNally.

Chen, H., & Rossi, P. H. (Eds.). (1992). *Using theory to improve program and policy evaluations*. New York: Greenwood.

Cochran, N. (1978). Grandma Moses and the "corruption" of data. *Evaluation Quarterly, 2,* 363-373.

Cohen, J. (1977). *Statistical power analysis for the behavioral sciences*. Hillsdale, NJ: Lawrence Erlbaum.

Cohen, J. (1988). *Statistical power analysis for the behavioral sciences* (2nd ed.). Hillsdale, NJ: Lawrence Erlbaum.

Committee on National Statistics, National Research Council. (1985). *Sharing research data*. Washington, DC: National Academy Press.

Cook, T. D., & Campbell, D. T. (1979). *Quasi-experimentation: Design and analysis issues for field settings*. Chicago: Rand McNally.

Cooper, H. M. (1989). *Integrating research: A guide for literature reviews* (2nd ed.). Newbury Park, CA: Sage.

Dennis, M. L. (1990). Assessing the validity of randomized field experiments: An example from drug treatment research. *Evaluation Review, 14,* 347-373.

Denzin, N. K. (1989). *Interpretive interactionism*. Newbury Park, CA: Sage.

DeVellis, R. F. (1991). *Scale development: Theory and applications*. Newbury Park, CA: Sage.

Devitt, C., Rog, D. J., & Bickman, L. (1981). *Retail crime in Evanston: Report of the needs assessment survey*. Prepared for the Evanston Police Department, Evanston, IL.

Doolittle, F., & Traeger, L. (1990). *Implementing the national JTPA study*. New York: Manpower Demonstration Research Corporation.

Dworkin, R. J. (1992). *Researching persons with mental illness*. Newbury Park, CA: Sage.

Fetterman, D. M. (1989). *Ethnography: Step by step*. Newbury Park, CA: Sage.

Fowler, F. J., Jr. (1988). *Survey research methods* (rev. ed.). Newbury Park, CA: Sage.

Fowler, F. J., Jr., & Mangione, T. W. (1989). *Standardized survey interviewing: Minimizing interviewer-related error*. Newbury Park, CA: Sage.

Goffman, E. (1959). *The presentation of self in everyday life*. Garden City, NY: Doubleday.

Grady, K .E., & Wallston, B. S. (1988). *Research in health care settings*. Newbury Park, CA: Sage.

Hedrick, T. (1986, October). *The interaction of politics and evaluation*. Paper presented at the annual meetings of the American Evaluation Association, Kansas City, MO.

Hedrick, T. E., & Shipman, S. (1988). Multiple questions require multiple designs: An evaluation of the 1981 changes to the AFDC program. *Evaluation Review, 12*(4), 427-448.

Henry, G. T. (1990). *Practical sampling*. Newbury Park, CA: Sage.

Herring, K. L. (Ed.). (1987). *APA guide to research support* (3rd ed.). Washington, DC: American Psychological Association.

Jacobson, N. S., & Truax, P. (1991). Clinical significance: A statistical approach to defining meaningful change in psychological research. *Journal of Consultation and Clinical Psychology, 59,* 12-19.

Johnson, E. L. (1988). *The design matrix and other strategies for improving the design process*. College Park, MD: U.S. General Accounting Office Technical Conference.

Joint Legislation Audit and Review Commission. (1986). *Deinstitutionalization and community services*. Report of the Joint Legislative Audit and Review Commission to the Governor and the General Assembly of Virginia, Richmond.

Jorgensen, D. L. (1989). *Participant observation: A methodology for human studies*. Newbury Park, CA: Sage.

Kelly, J. R., & McGrath, J. E. (1988). *On time and method*. Newbury Park, CA: Sage.

Kimmel, A. J. (1988). *Ethics and values in applied social research*. Newbury Park, CA: Sage.

Kraemer, H. C., & Thiemann, S. (1987). *How many subjects? Statistical power analysis in research*. Stanford, CA: Stanford University, Department of Psychiatry and Behavioral Sciences.

Krippendorf, K. (1980). *Content analysis: An introduction to its methodology.* Newbury Park, CA: Sage.

Lavrakas, P. J. (1987). *Telephone survey methods: Sampling, selection, and supervision.* Newbury Park, CA: Sage.

Levin, H. M. (1983). *Cost-effectiveness: A primer.* Newbury Park, CA: Sage.

Lipsey, M. W. (1990). *Design sensitivity.* Newbury Park, CA: Sage.

Lipsey, M. W., Crosse, S., Dunkle, J., Pollard, J., & Stobart, G. (1985). Evaluation: The state of the art and the sorry state of the science. *New Directions for Program Evaluation, 27,* 7-18.

Love, A. J. (1991). *Internal evaluation: Building organizations from within.* Newbury Park, CA: Sage.

Majchrzak, A. (1984). *Methods for policy research.* Newbury Park, CA: Sage.

Marín, G., & Marín, B. V. (1991). *Research with Hispanic populations.* Newbury Park, CA: Sage.

Maruyama, G., & Deno, S. (1992). *Research in educational settings.* Newbury Park, CA: Sage.

Moore, C. M. (1987). *Group techniques for idea building.* Newbury Park, CA: Sage.

Nagel, S. S., & Neef, M. (1979). *Policy analysis in social science research.* Newbury Park, CA: Sage.

Nagi, S. Z., & Corwin, R .G. (Eds.). (1972). *The social contexts of research.* New York: Wiley-Interscience.

Rog, D. J. (1985). *A methodological analysis of evaluability assessment.* Ph.D. dissertation, Vanderbilt University, Nashville, TN.

Rog, D. J. (in press). Expanding the boundaries of evaluation: Strategies for refining and evaluating ill-defined interventions. In S. L. Friedman & H. C. Haywood (Eds.), *Developmental followup: Concepts, genres, domains, and methods.* New York: Academic Press.

Rog, D. J., Andranovich, G. D., & Rosenblum, S. (1987). *Intensive case management for persons who are homeless and mentally ill: A review of community support program and human resource development program efforts* (3 vols.). Washington, DC: COSMOS Corporation.

Rog, D. J., & Bickman, L. (1984). The feedback research approach to evaluation: A method to increase evaluation utility. *Evaluation and Program Planning, 7,* 169-175. (Reprinted in Cordray, D. S., & Lipsey, M. W. (Eds.), *Evaluation Studies Review Annual, 11,* 1987)

Rog, D. J., & Henry, G. T. (1986, August). *A community profile of the deinstitutionalized.* Paper presented at the annual meeting of the American Psychological Association, Washington, DC.

Rog, D. J., & Henry, G. T. (1987). An implementation evaluation of community corrections. *Evaluation Review, 11,* 336-354.

Rog, D. J., & Huebner, R. (1992). Using research and theory in developing innovative programs for homeless individuals. In H. Chen & P. H. Rossi (Eds.), *Using theory to improve program and policy evaluations* (pp. 129-144). New York: Greenwood.

Rog, D. J., & Landis, J. (1985). *Evaluating secondary data.* Manual prepared for methods workshop with the Virginia Joint Legislative Audit and Review Commission, Richmond.

Rosenthal, R. (1984). *Meta-analytic procedures for social research.* Newbury Park, CA: Sage.

Rosenthal, R. (1991). *Meta-analytic procedures for social research* (rev. ed.). Newbury Park, CA: Sage.

Rossi, J. S. (1990). Statistical power of psychological research: What have we gained in twenty years? *Journal of Consulting and Clinical Psychology, 58*(5), 646-656.

Rutman, L. (1980). *Planning useful evaluations: Evaluability assessments.* Newbury Park, CA: Sage.

Scheirer, M. A. (1981). *Program implementation: The organizational context.* Newbury Park, CA: Sage.

Schmidt, R., Beyna, L., & Haar, J. (1982). Evaluability assessment: Principles and practice. In G. J. Stahler & W. R. Tash (Eds.), *Innovative approaches to mental health evaluation.* New York: Academic Press.

Schneider, A. L., & Darcy, R. E. (1984). Policy implications of using significant tests in evaluation research. *Evaluation Review, 8,* 573-582.

Schwandt, T. A., & Halpern, E. S. (1988). *Linking auditing and meta-evaluation: Enhancing quality in applied research.* Newbury Park, CA: Sage.

Sieber, J. E. (1992). *Planning ethically responsible research: A guide for students and internal review boards.* Newbury Park, CA: Sage.

Stewart, D. W. (1984). *Secondary research: Information sources and methods.* Newbury Park, CA: Sage.

Stewart, D. W., & Kamins, M. (in press). *Secondary research: Information sources and methods* (2nd ed.). Newbury Park, CA: Sage.

Stewart, D. W., & Shamdasani, P. N. (1990). *Focus groups: Theory and practice.* Newbury Park, CA: Sage.

Thompson, M. S. (1980). *Benefit-cost analysis for program evaluation.* Newbury Park, CA: Sage.

U.S. General Accounting Office. (1984a). *Designing evaluations: Methodology transfer paper 4* (PEMD, July). Washington, DC: Author.

U.S. General Accounting Office. (1984b). *An evaluation of the 1981 AFDC changes: Initial analyses* (GAO/PEMD, July 2). Washington, DC: Author.

U.S. General Accounting Office. (1985). *An evaluation of the 1981 AFDC changes: Final report* (GAO-PEMD-85-4). Washington, DC: Author.

U.S. General Accounting Office. (1988). *Stars and stripes: Inherent conflicts lead to allegations of military censorship* (GAO/NSIAD-89-60, December). Washington, DC: Author.

U.S. General Accounting Office. (1991). *Motorcycle helmet laws save lives and reduce costs to society* (GAO/RCED-91-170, July). Washington, DC: Author.

Weimer, D. L., & Vining, A. R. (1992). *Policy analysis: Concepts and practice.* Englewood Cliffs, NJ: Prentice-Hall.

Wholey, J. S. (1979). *Evaluation: Promise and performance.* Washington, DC: Urban Institute.

Wholey, J. S. (1987). Evaluability assessment: Developing program theory. In L. Bickman (Ed.), *Using program theory in evaluation. New directions for program evaluation, No. 33* (pp. 77-92). San Francisco: Jossey-Bass.

Yeaton, W. H., & Sechrest, L. (1987). No-difference research. *Evaluation Practice in Review, 34,* 67-82.

INDEX

About the Authors

Leonard Bickman is Director of the Center for Mental Health Policy at Vanderbilt University. He is Professor of Psychology and Public Policy at George Peabody College, and a Professor of Psychiatry at the Vanderbilt School of Medicine, as well as Director of the Social Psychology Graduate Program at Peabody College. He has conducted major evaluation studies for foundations and federal and state governments. He currently is directing a large-scale evaluation of an innovative children's mental health system that is supported by a grant from the National Institute of Mental Health and a contract from the U.S. Army. He is coeditor of the Sage Applied Social Research Methods Series and on the editorial board of *New Directions in Evaluation*. He is a former president of the Society for the Psychological Study of Social Issues, and a Fellow of the American Psychological Association. His fellowships and awards include the City College of New York Distinguished Alumni Award for Outstanding Contributions to the Advancement of Psychology; The Forchheimer Visiting Professor fellowship at the Hebrew University of Jerusalem; the American Psychological Association Award for Distinguished Contributions to Education and Training in Psychology; and the Peabody Faculty Excellence Award.

Terry E. Hedrick is Director of the Training Institute of the U.S. General Accounting Office (GAO). In this role, she directs agency training and education efforts to prepare GAO staff to carry out their responsibilities to produce quality and unbiased audit, evaluation, and policy analysis work for Congress. During a 15-year career, she has conducted and managed program evaluation work for state and county government, the federal government, and the private sector. After receiving her doctorate in social psychology from the University of Missouri and completing a postdoctoral appointment in program evaluation methods at Northwestern University, she spent two years as Assistant Professor in Psychology at Kent State University. Subsequently she was selected to serve as a Staff Associate in Employment Policy at The Brookings Institution and held appointments in the evaluation offices in the Employment and Training Administration, Department of Labor, and the Food and Nutrition Service, Department of Agriculture. She previously spent 5 years with the GAO in the early 1980s as part of the Program Evaluation and Methodology Division, followed by experience in the private sector with COSMOS Corporation and Abt Associates. Throughout her career, she has been especially interested in the problems associated with bringing rigorous and unbiased applied research approaches to complex social issues.

Debra J. Rog directs the Washington Office of the Vanderbilt University Center for Mental Health Policy and holds a Research Assistant Professorship in the Department of Public Policy. She currently is the principal investigator of an evaluation of The Robert Wood Johnson Foundation/Department of Housing and Urban Development Homeless Families Program, a nine-city demonstration project focused on establishing comprehensive service systems for homeless families with multiple problems. Other current areas of research involve services-enriched housing, children's mental health, and knowledge dissemination. Prior to joining Vanderbilt, she served as Associate Director in the National Institute of Mental Health Office of Programs for the Homeless Mentally Ill, where she was responsible for developing and implementing research and evaluation activities. She also is a recognized research methodologist, with publications and papers in the areas of applied social research and program evaluation, and has served as coeditor of the Sage Applied Social Research Methods Series since its inception.

The views expressed in this book are those of the authors only and should not be construed to represent the policies or position of the U.S. General Acounting Office.